To Bob & Sylvia,

Fellow intuitives

& friends!

Kathryn Harwig

the *intuitive* advantage

the *intuitive*
advantage

Kathryn Harwig

Spring Press
Minneapolis, Minnesota

Printed in the United States of America
Book design and composition: Dorie McClelland

Publisher's Cataloging-in-Publication Data
Harwig, Kathryn, 1951–
    The intuitive advantage
      1. Intuition (Psychology).   2. Spiritual Life.
      I. Title

BF 311.H 2000

                  153.4'4
                  dc21

ISBN 0-9638822-3-6

contents

intuition: your sixth sense

"God's punishment is quicker than men's." My mother used that phrase a lot when I was growing up, usually when I stubbed a toe or had some other small accident. I never quite understood what I had done that called for punishment, but I knew it couldn't be good. Much of the time it seemed to do with speaking the truth as I saw it. Children in the 1950's were meant to be seen and not heard. I was shy enough for that to be fine with me, but I had this inner knowledge that sometimes demanded to be shared. However, I quickly learned that intuitive ability wasn't something to be advertised. Intuitive knowing was considered suspect, sinful, or just plain crazy in my small Minnesota town in the 1950's.

Until just recently intuitive ability in our society has been ignored, discounted, trivialized and in some cases criminalized. Many people claim that intuition doesn't even exist, that the "accidental" happenings of gut instinct or psychic know-ing are lies-things made up to make oneself feel better. Those who believe in intuition have been forced to meet in back rooms and secret societies and to feel ashamed to admit these activities to friends and neighbors. No wonder most people don't use intuition as a helpful tool in everyday life. Not only have people not been taught how to use intuition; they have been told it doesn't exist! Only recently has intuition become a subject worthy of serious study. As our society becomes increasingly technologically complex its members are growing more and more intuitively gifted. It is now the time for the human race to claim its intuitive birthright.

Intuitive ability is very much like musical ability—every-one has some musical talent, but very few people can sit down and play the piano without training. Music occurs naturally in the world, but it is not a thing that can be touched or felt. Music is created when people believe in it, trust their abilities and are taught the rules. Similarly, everyone has the capability to be intuitive, but very few are natural born psychics. As with musical ability, the key to training intuition is to believe in it, discover our strengths, learn the rules, and then practice, prac-tice, practice. One of the goals of this book is to give you tools with which to practice and time in which to develop confi-dence in your own ability.

Although all children are born as natural intuitives, they are carefully, if not intentionally, taught what to see and what to pay attention to in this world. This teaching comes very early, from parents, friends, teachers, and, of course, the media.

People are told what society considers real and what it does not, what to focus attention upon and what to disregard. If society taught people to ignore music in this fashion, it would soon not be heard by anyone. Instead, musical senses are nurtured while intuitive ability is discounted, ridiculed and ignored. This conformity may be necessary for societal cohesion, but it comes at a great price. To enhance intuition people must regain that sense of wonder and magic that was once a part of everyone's childhood.

As a child, I was lucky to retain much of my natural intuitive ability, although at the time I would not have considered myself fortunate. Asthma and a difficulty in swallowing ravaged my childhood. During the 1950's asthmatic children like me were kept still. Movement was thought to exacerbate my symptoms, so I was excused from all physical activity. I missed most of the first grade because I was too sick to tolerate a full day of school. I spent my nights propped up in a sitting position because I couldn't breathe while lying down.

My parents were very poor with few resources for babysitters or medical care. When I was about six, our local town doctor told my mother that I would surely die if we didn't move to Arizona. (It was believed that the warm desert air cured asthma.) Acting as if I was deaf, they held this conversation in front of me. "Surely we'll move," I thought to myself. Every day I would wait for the packing to begin, but finally I realized we weren't going to leave Minnesota. I waited to die. After a while, I concluded that wasn't going to happen either. With that, I realized I couldn't believe much of what adults said. I decided to trust my own inner knowing. I've never truly changed my mind about that.

I was, by all accounts, a strange child. I couldn't ride a bike, throw a ball, or run. I had no interest in dolls or toys and had few friends. I taught myself to read very young and spent all of my time with my "face in a book," as my mother would say. I also developed an unexplainable fascination with people's hands. By the time I was four years old, I had discovered that I could learn about people by looking at their palms. The lines, particularly those in the hands of my grandmother's elderly friends, fascinated me. "Look," I would say to them while pointing to a line, "this is when you got married and these are your children." I was surprised that they couldn't see what to me was in plain sight.

I didn't have a clue as to what I was doing at that time and for some time people thought it was cute. When I became older, they decided it was spooky and I was encouraged to stop. However, by that time I was hooked. I asked our local librarian for books on palmistry. I learned the names of the lines and the standard interpretations. Then I decided what was true based on my innermost knowing. Kids at school would let me practice on them until their parents found out. I also learned that I could "sneak peeks" at people's hands when they weren't looking and, finally, I learned that I could sometimes know all I wanted just by turning my attention toward the person, even if I couldn't see the hands.

In retrospect, I believe that my self-taught intuitive training was invaluable. As a result of my illness and unusual behavior, I was left pretty much alone. I was quiet enough that people usually ignored me, which was generally all right with me. I would study them, figuring out their stories, "making up" their histories. It was a hobby I could do without much movement or need for companionship.

My family had a love-hate relationship with intuition. Astrology and all things mystical fascinated my mother, but we belonged to a fundamentalist Christian church which taught that such things were of the devil. I was told by the church that fortune telling and psychic ability were evil, yet my experience was that these things were good and helpful. As a result, it seemed prudent to keep my ideas and experiences to myself.

My mother would periodically purchase OUIJA boards which she would use until she became so frightened by what she learned that she would burn them. By the time I was old enough to hold the board, we discovered that it worked best for me. The plastic pointer would fly between the letters so fast that we were unable to interpret the meaning. I would "work" the board by myself, with my older sister sitting next to me calling out the letters, and my mother writing them down as they were called out. Later, when the marker would fall dead of its own accord, we would try to decipher the sentences and discern the meaning of the message.

The first time we burned the board was after it predicted the assassination of John F. Kennedy. The second was when it told of the deaths of several family members in a car crash. Each time the predictions came true, my mother would ask the Lord for forgiveness and destroy the board. Finally, I refused to do it any more. I didn't care for the furor of the process. I much preferred to trust my inner knowing, even though I hadn't named it as such.

Incidents like these convinced me that life was not as it seemed. Perhaps because I was sick for so much of my childhood, life itself had a somewhat surreal quality. I remember a vivid vision I had as a tiny child. In this vision I sat with an older woman looking at a large and beautifully illustrated storybook. As we watched, my life was shown in the book, happening as if it were fiction. I was clearly taught that what I took to be "life" was, in reality, just a story. Life, as I then knew it, was like a play or a movie that I could step back from and observe at another level. Since that lesson, I have on occasion used this method to separate myself from life's happenings. Just as when I was a small child, this technique illustrates to me that what I believe to be reality is, at most, a tiny piece of a very large puzzle. This knowledge is both comforting and terrifying. I also believe it completely.

Long before most people had heard of the metaphysical, my family was reading (and burning) books about walk-ins, astrology, and channeling. My mother's cousin Elwood would mail us books and visit once or twice a year to charm me with stories about pyramids and aliens. Sometimes we'd even go out searching for UFOs. Even though we never saw one, his open mind and his quest for the truth impressed me. He lived in New York City at the time, a long way from the conservative, strongly religious small-town atmosphere in which I lived. My fondest dream was to get away, to go to a place where I fit in, where I could feel normal. Where I could, perhaps, even talk about my ideas and experiences without being afraid of being burned myself.

I believe that because of my unusual childhood, I wasn't taught to filter out intuitive knowledge the way that most children are. While I certainly would never recommend this way of developing intuition, it was effective in my case. Then, when I turned twelve years of age, my asthma mysteriously disappeared and I spent many years attempting "to be normal" and ignoring my intuitive skills. With my health restored, the veil between the spiritual and physical worlds turned into a solid locked door. I worked very hard to think and act like my peers. I wanted more than anything else to do the things that other people did such as physical activities and sports, dating and socializing. I dreamed of getting married and having a career. What I did not want to be was a mystic. For once, I was determined to "fit in." For a few years I used palmistry as a party game. Then, in an effort to conform to the world, I consciously attempted to forget the visions and the gifts.

I spent nearly twenty years on my quest for normality. I finished college, majoring in psychology in a misguided attempt to figure out what was "wrong" with me. All I really learned was an efficient way to train white rats, a skill I have had very little need for in my adult life. I married a kind, gentle, and "normal" man, and together we bought a split-level house in an average suburb. On the outside, I seemed to have accomplished my goal: I was as stereotypically middle-American as you could get.

On the inside, however, I still felt like a freak. I would awaken with the awful feeling that I'd forgotten to do something terribly important. My dreams were full of symbolism, deadlines missed, unkept promises. I worked at that time as a probation officer, interviewing convicted felons and writing reports about their history and crime for the Court. I was very good at it. I knew, without asking, their innermost fears, and their motivations. I also knew they were not all that much different from me. Within all people there are only two motivating emotions—love and fear. The convicted offenders with whom I worked had chosen to act out of their fear, rather than their love. But, even the most heinous of crimes was committed by a person who contained kernels of love. Someday I hoped to be able to teach people to see and act upon the emotion of compassion rather than of terror.

In the meantime, I had to deal with my own emotions and fear. "What could I do," I wondered, "that would make me feel confident and self-assured?" I looked around the courthouse and saw a group of people who seemed fearless. I wanted to be like them—so I went to law school.

I discovered, of course, that inside most lawyers is a quivering mass of insecurity, but by that time it was too late. I soon became immersed in a sea of contracts and torts. I still worked full time as a probation officer while attending law school four nights a week. Weekends were devoted to studying. There was no time for things of the spirit, nor any time for introspection. I learned that staying very busy quieted the nagging voice of intuition. In fact, if the pace of life is frantic enough, that whisper may even become inaudible for a time. I would soon learn that ignoring the voice would cause it to return with a shout.

My husband had enrolled in law school at the same time, which conveniently kept any domestic issues from surfacing as well. We kept up that pace for nearly four years. Then, six weeks prior to our graduation from law school, my life took an irrevocable turn. My husband and I were having a rare meal at home together when I felt a sudden and intense pain in my chest. Unable to trace a cause, I waited until the pain was unbearable before Loren rushed me screaming to the emergency room.

I spent the last six weeks of my law school education in the intensive care unit. Although I was allowed to graduate with my class, I never returned to the school. The perforated esophagus that had almost taken my life would change me in ways I would not fully appreciate until years of pain, frustration, addiction, and despair had passed.

Until the day when my esophagus perforated I had spent my adult life striving for the future. Vacations, family, hobbies, everything I allegedly valued had been delayed for the sake of my goal to be a lawyer. I had always believed that someday it would pay off and I would have the time and money to make up for all the delayed pleasures. Then, without any warning, I found myself lying in a hospital bed while feeding tubes pumped in nutrients, antibiotics, and painkillers and chest tubes pumped out toxins and infection. My goal then became surviving until the next shot of morphine. My biggest achievement was the day I was able to sit up by myself.

My esophagus had perforated without warning. I had suffered from swallowing difficulties since I was a child, but had always been told it was due to "nerves." It would later be discovered that I had a condition known as Barrett's esophagus, which caused ulcer-like sores to gradually eat holes through tissue. But that night, my condition did not appear serious enough to get the attention it truly deserved. We were met in the emergency room by a bored intern who instructed me to swallow malt-sized cups of barium for X-rays of my digestive tract. Unable to find the obstruction he anticipated, he inserted a NG tube down my nose, gave me a shot of Demerol, checked me into a hospital bed and returned to his crossword puzzle. The next morning, my chest cavity had filled with air, hardened barium, and infection. I looked as if I had been injected with helium. Amazingly, the staff didn't appear to notice. I was placed in a wheelchair and taken to a clinic nearby. The esophageal specialist turned pale the minute he saw me. He rushed from the room and came back a few minutes later with a chest surgeon. I knew, from the look of panic on their faces, that something was terribly wrong.

Wishing to consult privately, they wheeled me into a small storage room adjacent to the examining room. I sat in the wheelchair and felt my life force weaken. Suddenly, I noticed that I was observing the room from a different perspective. My vision had a vividness I had never before experienced.

Everything was much clearer and brighter. Even though I didn't have my glasses on, I could see perfectly. I looked down from my new vantage point to see a rather pathetic sight. I observed my body scrunched down in the wheelchair, no longer able to support itself upright. It looked gray, very sick, very sad, and very pitiful. I realized with some surprise that that was me. I also realized I was dying. And I discovered that I didn't care. I had no more attachment to that body than I would have to a pair of discarded and worn-out shoes.

Leaving my body behind, I left the room. While traveling near ceiling level, I proceeded to the area where the two doctors were consulting frantically. I could tell they were alarmed by my condition. I watched impassively as they desperately discussed various options for my care. The emergency doctor, they feared, had totally mis-diagnosed my condition. They were concerned that he might have inserted the NG tube through the hole in my esophagus and into my chest rather than down into my stomach. The barium that I had swallowed the night before had escaped into my chest cavity where it had hardened overnight into a cement-like substance which encased some of my internal organs. I listened to their conversation without alarm. I knew that if they didn't do something immediately, the body in the other room would die. I also knew without any uncertainty that it simply did not matter. I have never felt such a peace. The next day I awoke in the recovery room after emergency chest and stomach surgery. The doctors had saved my life.

After six weeks in the hospital, I returned home to study

for the bar examination. Amazingly, I passed the test with flying colors. Despite my illness, my husband and I set up a law practice near our home. On the surface, I had not only survived, I had accomplished all of my goals. But none of them seemed very important anymore. Becoming a lawyer had been a goal I had striven towards for four long years—perhaps all my adult life. I had lived my life on a timetable with the unwavering belief that if I worked hard, studied hard and saved money, I would somehow achieve that nameless, faceless calling that haunted me in those rare quiet moments when I actually stopped working.

For five years after my illness, I lived in a shadow land of chronic pain and addiction to painkillers while struggling to recover from three chest and stomach surgeries. All of the things I had strived so hard to achieve seemed laughable in the face of incessant pain and physical disability. My out-of-body experience had lessened my fear of death but had done little for my fear of life. I knew that I had changed, but I didn't know how. Nothing was important any more. I'd become a lawyer. It was a good job, but I knew it wasn't my calling. It was how I made my living, not how I lived. How could I be proud of becoming a lawyer when I now knew that life was tenuous at best? I had faced death squarely and seen that nothing mattered. But where did I go from there?

Gradually, as the pain became manageable and the narcotics dropped their hold on my soul, I re-entered life. But I wasn't the same person. I developed an over-riding passion to experience the world. I changed from being a woman who had barely left the state of Minnesota to a person who spent much of her disposable cash and time traveling the globe. I felt driven to see and to do things that I'd previously had no interest in experiencing.

I had lived when I should have died and, as a result, would never look at life the same again. My near-death experience caused a life metamorphosis that left me with different values, ideas, and a heightened sense of mystery and intuition. I could no longer deny who or what I was. I could no longer pretend that the gifts I had been given were valueless. I entered upon a quest for myself. And as soon as I started using my intuitive gifts again, my life changed. I no longer wondered what I had forgotten; I knew what I was to do.

Ten years after starting my law firm, I began teaching and training on intuitive development. As a practicing attorney with a successful firm in a small conservative suburb of Minneapolis, I was somewhat concerned about what teaching intuition classes would do to my reputation. Still, I had "come out of the closet" a few years before with the publication of my first book on palmistry. Once I'd been billed as the "palm-reading lawyer" on television, print, and radio, teaching intuition appeared almost reputable. Even though I knew that the acceptance of and interest in intuition in society was changing, I was still surprised at the positive reception given to my training programs. Within a few months of offering my first class, I was being called to train police, teachers, secretaries, corrections workers, and business and professional people. Many in these groups were skeptical, but all were curious. The feedback I have received over the years during which I have taught these sessions, tells me that people are hungry for ways to improve their intuition. As a world, people have reached a point where they know, at a deep inner level, that it is time to reclaim their intuitive heritage.

The dictionary's definition of intuition is simple. It is a direct knowing or learning of something without the conscious use of reasoning. It is those times when we know who is on the telephone before we answer it, when we feel uneasy and unsettled before something happens, when we easily and unknowingly drive right to the only parking space in a full lot. It happens to us all the time. I have never met a person who has not had such experiences, although I have met many people who explain the experiences away as being coincidental or a self-fulfilling prophecy.

At some level, few of us deny the reality of intuition. Life experiences verify its existence. But knowing how to use it at command is an entirely different thing. Intuition is meant to be used—just like any other gift. It is meant to be developed and wants to be trained. The claim that intuition "just happens" is no more than a myth. In this book I will debunk that myth and provide concrete and practical ways to develop and train intuition. Intuition can become a regular, reliable, controllable, and predictable tool that can be used by everyone.

I have created this training program to give you the opportunity to practice all different types of intuitive techniques. You may find that some come easily while others are more difficult and you will prefer certain ones. This is supposed to happen. No one will become an expert at all the intuitive practices—nor do they need to be. You will learn what works for you; and you are encouraged to discard the rest. However, it is important to try all the techniques. Everyone is unique, and intuition speaks to each person in a different manner. If you don't try all the exercises, you may miss just the one that will work best for you!

This book has been laid out as a six-month training course. I recognize, of course, that many, if not most, of you will read the book quickly and then use what you find most interesting. I understand this behavior; but in my experience, it is not the best way to learn to be intuitive. Mastering intuition takes time, just like all other skill development. It is best done in an orderly basis with a proper amount of attention. The best use of this program may very well be to do it with a partner or group where you get encouragement and support. Your intuition will tell you how best to use the information in this book. Do one exercise or all of them. Read it in one night or over six months. Trust your intuition to lead you on the best course.

My goal is to give you a method of developing a partnership between your logical and your intuitive abilities. You will not be asked to throw away your analytical mind (although you will be asked to put it aside on occasion). You will be taught to use both sides of your brain, giving you an advantage in all areas of your life—the intuitive advantage!

1

developing focus

What is the most important thing you can do to develop your intuition? If I had to name one thing it would be to learn how intuition speaks to you and then practice, practice, practice. Often, people are disappointed when I tell them this. They want a secret mantra or code that will endow them with immediate effortless mystical abilities. It just doesn't work that way. In my experience, everything I am really good at I can do because I work at it. Practice is important in my music, my law practice, my writing, even in my relationships.

This doesn't mean that intuition isn't fun. Actually, practicing intuition is a great way to enjoy your day. Intuition training for me is a wonderful game that keeps me from getting bored or impatient. When I am in a potentially dull situation, I create intuitive games to play with myself. For example, I recently went to court on a real estate matter with several million dollars at stake. That sort of case tends to attract lots of lawyers and takes way too much time. To keep myself awake, I practiced my intuition by "predicting" things—how many lawyers would be in the courtroom, what color suits would they wear (gray is always a good guess), who would speak first, who would speak next, how many times would the judge yawn, and so forth.

I also keep an intuitive log where I track my hits and misses. This gives me some statistics for those of you who are fond of them. For example, I am about 75% accurate at predicting which elevator will come, but only around 60% accurate about who's on the phone. My accuracy in finding parking places is increasing rapidly. I recommend that you start this program by creating an intuitive diary or journal where you log your practices, keep statistics, and record your exercises. A simple three ring binder is sufficient, or you can use a beautiful blank book. You can stick plain pieces of paper into a folder if you prefer. The structure and image you create is up to you. Take time to think of what it is that will give you joy. Your intuition diary will make for some fascinating reading as your intuitive journey continues.

Before intuition will be of value to you, you truly have to believe it exists. No one will practice something very long if they don't believe in it. This week you will be learning focus. As you do that, you may also experience memories of how intuition has felt to you in the past. Take some time this week to recall instances in your life when you have used intuition or had what felt like psychic flashes. You will also be asked to observe, but not attempt to elicit, intuitive events as they happen this week. (Yes, there will be such events.) This is not as simple an assignment as it may first appear. You must first suspend your disbelief and self-doubt. Remember what it felt like to be a child, how you "just knew" when your parents weren't getting along or when you would have a fight with your best friend. Did you ever tell your parents you were sick because you knew it would be bad day at school? Consider the possibility that you really did know what the day would be like.

When you recall an intuitive instance, recreate that experience in your mind. How did it show itself? Did you feel it in your stomach or your neck? Did you get a picture in your mind? Did you have a strong thought? Make a note of when you were intuitive and the way that intuition spoke to you. Intuition speaks differently to all of us. You may be more likely to get a feeling than a thought or vice-versa. Discovering your most common method of intuition will help you to recognize it the next time it occurs. Remember as many instances as you can, the earlier in time the better.

Many times when I ask people to volunteer intuitive moments in their lives, they tell me about predicting catastrophes. The most common story I hear is of knowing about a person's death at or before the time it happened. This is a very powerful example of intuitive ability. But, the problem is, the person usually ends the story by saying, "And I never want that to happen again." Of course, if being intuitive only involved the prediction of disaster, no one would want that skill, particularly if there is no ability to change the outcome. While intuition may sometimes provide this sort of information, it is not the aim of the intuitive advantage. Rather, the use of intuition should make life better, not just scary. I want you to remember the ordinary moments of intuition—the time you walked into a new classroom and were drawn to sit next to your now best friend, or when you had a feeling that a particular highway was under construction. This is the type of knowing that will improve the quality of your life. After all, what good does it do to be intuitive if you don't know when the bus is going to be late?

If you can't remember any times of being intuitive, talk to others about their memories. Watch those around you, particularly children. Watching children can give you many insights into your own childhood. Notice how a baby might suddenly start to cry when someone walks into a room. Ask yourself if the baby picked up something about the person or her mood. Ask yourself how *you* felt when that person arrived.

Still can't remember any intuitive moments? How about a time when you knew what was in a present before you opened it. Do you ever know who's on the phone before you pick it up? Can you remember feeling a sense of dread before a meeting during which everything went wrong? Or, conversely, how about the days when you wake up "on top of the world" and the day goes by easily. Are these coincidences or did you know how the day would go ahead of time? Allow yourself to consider that as a possibility.

Write down at least three or four memories of intuitive

happenings. If you have a friend on a similar path, share your memories with each other—perhaps prompting each of you to remember even more psychic instances. Have fun with your intuitive memories and claim them as your own. Recreate the feelings until you can truly say, "I am an intuitive."

Once you realize that you are intuitive, you will want to develop ways to use your intuition, instead of letting it use you. The first crucial element of intuition training is that of intention. Imagine living your life without intention. You would get up in the morning when you awoke with no plans or schedule. Perhaps, if the telephone rang or someone came to the door, you would react to these events, allowing life to happen to you and take you where it wished. This is perhaps, how some of us act on a weekend or holiday, but few of us live our day-to-day lives in such a fashion. Very little would get accomplished in a world in which we allowed our lives to happen to us, rather than structuring or planning them. While an unstructured life has appeal to me, I know that to live the way I wish and do the things I love, I need to plan rather than react, schedule instead of respond.

Yet when it comes to intuition, we tend to let it "just happen." When I tell people that I train intuition, the most common response is "How can you train intuition? I thought it was something that just came to me." This misconception keeps us from even attempting to bring this skill under our command.

Our society is so primitive when it comes to intuition that we are similar to the stoneage people who believed that fire was something that just happened, a powerful and frightening occurrence that was beyond their control. I can envision a group of my distant ancestors marveling at the majesty and beauty of a raging fire, perhaps caused by a lightning strike. From afar, they could perhaps even appreciate how useful fire could be, imagine how warmth and cooking ability would aid their lives. But, until they could access and control fire, it remained terrifying and unmanageable—something to be feared rather than used as a tool.

We are in the stone age of our intuitive lives. From afar we view our own and other's psychic events and react in fear or awe. Because unintentional intuitive events happen without warning, they seem to rage through our lives, often causing more havoc than help. For intuition to be of value, we must learn to control it. It belongs to us and we govern and command it. It is not a frightening out-of-control event. Claim your right to use intuition. If you are in circumstance where you wish additional information, intend that you receive it.

This morning when I sat down at my computer, I not only expected that it would work, I also turned it on, went to the right program, and started to type. If I had merely sat in front of it, wishing words to magically appear, I would have soon become convinced that computers "don't work." Maybe I would have quit in disgust, thinking that there really isn't such a thing as a word processing system. I would have picked up my pen and promised myself I'd never play with such a mysterious thing again. From then on I would hand-write everything! Many of us act this way when it comes to intuition. We may make a half-hearted attempt to be intuitive, but we don't know enough to push the execute button. Then we walk away thinking intuition doesn't really exist or, at least, that we don't know how to use it.

In order to make intuition a usable tool in your life, you need to know how to turn it on and where to find the execute button. There are many ways to do this, but the best way that I know of is to intentionally enter into a focus state. In a focus state, we reduce the number of high-amplitude Beta brainwaves that form the constant mental chatter we carry on in our minds. Research has shown that an average person has twelve or more independent thoughts every minute of every day. In my classes, I ask students to watch their thoughts for one minute and count each separate thought. Those who are able to do so have reported as many as forty separate thoughts in a one-minute period! If one of these thoughts were an intuitive message, how many people would recognize it? The goal of learning to focus is to reduce this verbal mind chatter to a manageable level and allow some space for your intuitive mind to speak to you. Your intuition is very powerful but it often speaks in a whisper, while your conscious analytical mind is a loud-mouthed dictator.

My favorite way of creating an almost instantaneous focus state is to relax my tongue. Take a minute right now and try this exercise. When people talk to themselves, they tend to move their tongue. If you concentrate on relaxing your tongue, you make it almost impossible for this sub-vocalization to occur. When you reduce your mental ruminating, you create room for intuition to speak.

Each of you must find your own best way of relaxing your tongue. I imagine my tongue floating in my mouth while I let my chin drop and my jaw loosen. Once you have mastered this technique, you can loosen your tongue in a matter of seconds. This exercise puts me in a very mild trance state in which my brainwaves are altered from high speed Beta waves to a slower Alpha state. In this altered consciousness, I am much more accessible to intuitive messages. I practice tongue loosening many times a day. I often use a trigger, such as a ringing telephone, to remind me to practice. Then, I may ask myself who is calling before I pick up the line. Loosening my tongue also helps me in times when I am feeling tense or angry, and is quite effective when I am having difficulty sleeping. It may make a difference in your life if you try it.

Some of my students hate this exercise. They report having even more thoughts or tell me that all they can think about is whether they are loosening their tongue correctly. As with everything I teach, if this doesn't work for you, throw it away. You may need to find another focus activity such as watching your breath or concentrating on a flame or other object. It doesn't matter what you use or how you do it, as long as it works for you.

You may have noticed that you get intuitive thoughts while driving, bathing, running, or other such activities. That is because these sorts of activities often induce trance states, where your Beta mindwaves slow down and leave space for your intuition. You can encourage more intuitive thoughts by asking for them before you begin these things. For example, if you are a runner who is frequently "in the zone," don't distract yourself by listening to music or talking. Rather, tell yourself that you are open to intuitive thoughts while running, then run as usual. The same is true when you drive. Many of us "trance drive," often arriving at our destination without any memory of the trip. This is good news-bad news for our society. I am convinced that much of the aggressive behavior on our roads is caused because when in a trance we become more of who we already are. Our true natures, hopes, and fears are revealed to us, and for some of us that is a terrifying thing. Without understanding why, we then become aggressive, angry, and rude.

Recently I read an interview of a driver who had been arrested after running another car off the road because the other driver had "cut in front of him." This person claimed that the whole incident had "seemed like a dream—not quite real." He went on to say that he hadn't really understood what he had done until he found himself standing in a ditch looking at the other car.

We are responsible for our behavior, even when in a trance. We can program ourselves to drive serenely, accepting our intuitive thoughts and lowering our aggressive instincts. Recognizing your own focus activities and trance states will give you control over them. They are not induced by anything or anyone other than you. If you practice focusing you will gain greater control of not only your intuition but also your emotions and behavior.

A focus activity is one that you can only do by fully concentrating on the task at hand. The classic focus activity is meditation. Meditation, like many spiritual practices, is both extremely simple and very difficult. It is simple in that all meditation truly entails is full and complete concentration. It is difficult because quieting the mind is a challenging thing to do. If you decide to start meditating, you can join a meditation group, center, or church where it is practiced. Tapes can aid in concentration and focus, or you can simply find a quiet time and a place without disturbances and begin to focus on your breath. Concentrate on its feel as it enters your nostrils. Notice how one nostril breathes more freely than the other. Observe the cool spot at the bottom of your throat. Breathe deeply from your diaphragm and concentrate on how your stomach and chest expand.

I find that staring at a flame or candle helps in my meditative practice. You may discover that repeating a word or mantra will help to focus the mind. The important part is to quiet your thoughts. You may only be able to do this for five minutes a day. That is enough. Do not let meditation become a burden or a task. Its purpose is to make you free, not to become another chore.

For many of us, meditation may not fit our basic personality. Some people become so frustrated by their inability to quiet their mind that they quit meditating after a very short time. However, there are many other activities that demand focus. For me, playing the piano is an easy way to clear my mind. I am incapable of worrying or thinking about anything else when I play.

Think of the activities in your life where you are fully present. Any pursuit that demands your total concentration is a focus activity for you. It may be sports, computers, playing an instrument, or making love. Whatever it is, the hallmark of the activity is its ability to get you away from the ruminations of your brain. Watching television, reading, talking to your family, or working generally do not qualify as focus activities. They all have that capability, of course, but usually they do not challenge the mind enough to demand its total attention. That is why you can spend an evening watching TV without feeling relaxed, or read a chapter of a novel only to realize you do not remember the plot. Your brain has been otherwise engaged in worry, projection, and fear.

Focus activities relax the brain by allowing it to be engaged rather than wandering aimlessly. Any focus activity will help you along your spiritual path by allowing you to experience the bliss of mindfulness.

Your assignment for this week is to practice various ways to find focus. Use the tongue-loosening technique, stare at a candle, and watch your breath. Promise yourself that you will practice focusing for at least ten minutes or more a day. If you get intuitive thoughts during this time, be aware of them, but do not encourage them. Simply note them in your intuitive diary. If you have memories of past intuitive events jot them down as well. Once you have developed a reliable method of focusing, you are well on your way to becoming a master intuitive. You may have discovered that you feel more peaceful, relaxed, and serene. This is a wonderful side effect of intuitive practices. They frequently cause you to slow down, sleep better, and take life in stride. Enjoy this week and remember to focus!

2

creating silence
and sacred space

"If you sit very quietly and look out of the corner of your eye," my grandfather whispered, "you might just see a fairy." We were a peculiar pair, Grandpa and I. I was a sickly child, unable to run and play with the other children, and he was known as the town "eccentric," a man with a booming voice and a gentle manner who never could hold a job or fit in with what passed for society in the small Minnesota town of Hinckley. Nobody could ever really tell me what was wrong with Grandpa, only that he had returned from World War I by way of what they called a sanitarium. Since then, he had had lots of time to sit quietly and watch fairies.

Grandpa and I would walk to the Grindstone River, across the dirt road from my grandparent's tiny farm. After we reached the riverbed, we turned to the right and went up a small bluff to a hidden knoll. It was filled with ferns and lichen-covered rocks. Grandpa taught me to search for the johnny-jump-ups, lilies-of-the-valley and jack-in-the-pulpits that were hidden amid the fallen logs and ancient stones. It was truly a mystical place, where it seemed only right to talk in whispers. It was our secret spot, where our club of two would hold weekly meetings. Sitting was one of Grandpa's best skills, or at least that's what Grandma always said. He taught me to sit for hours, looking at the glade with "gentle eyes." I learned to unfocus my sharp young vision until the green of the ferns melted and flowed into the shimmering of the air. And then, when the only sound was my own breath, I saw my first fairy.

Fairies are shy creatures. Grandpa said they were curious and couldn't help but come to see why such huge creatures were in their world. "But," he said, "you never look directly at a fairy. They are very private and hide their mysteries beneath their wings." The fairies were our special secret, Grandpa said. Seeing them was a reward for being still. "Only very unique people like us," he said, "would have the patience or the time to catch a glimpse of their veiled world." I agreed. Even at five years of age, I was quite certain no one would believe that I had actually seen fairies. And, of course, I already knew that no one listened to Grandpa at all.

I kept the secret of the fairies so well that, by the time I was an adult, I had completely forgotten about them. Only recently, when a friend was telling me about a movie she had seen about fairies, did I remember my very own fairy tale. Did I really see fairies so many years ago? I can't honestly say. Childhood memories are slippery things. I do know that the hours Grandpa and I sat in the fairy glade taught me the value of three things—silence, sacred space, and focus.

Our society has become so busy that the act of sitting silently is considered an aberration. "Being busy" is a very strong value. Look at the way we talk to each other. Shortly after the obligatory (at least in Minnesota) "How are you?" we explain in great detail the extreme franticness of our lives. If you don't believe this, try to engage in a conversation in which you do not say or hear the word "busy." It is close to impossible. Being busy is a badge of honor in America, and conversely, sitting quietly is looked down upon. No wonder so few adults see fairies!

How much time do you spend in silence? If you are like most of us, total quiet probably makes you uncomfortable. We have trained ourselves to expect a level of noise in our lives and we become anxious in silent situations. As a matter of fact, total silence has nearly been eliminated from our world. Recently a recording company attempted to record only natural noises such as rainfall, birds chirping, waterfalls, and the ocean. They had great difficulty finding anywhere in the world where they could record these sounds without human generated noises being heard in the distance. I find this tragic.

Most people report that their intuition speaks to them best when they are in a quiet, stress-free environment. The goal, of course, is to claim the intuitive advantage—to make intuition our tool that we can use anywhere—noisy, stressful, or not. When beginning to practice intuition, however, it helps to create a space of silence and serenity. It is much easier to listen to the still small voice of intuition if loud music, arguments, or commercials do not distract you.

Before you can truly start any intuitive practice you need to carve out time, silence, and space. None of the exercises in this book need huge chunks of your time. They are meant to be done in small segments and to be incorporated into your daily life. But you cannot do them in a business-as-usual fashion. This week, examine your life. Find the quiet times that exist in even the busiest of lives and claim them for your own. Create a sacred space, even if it is just a spot on your sofa, where you can be alone, peaceful, and intuitive.

First, take some time to do a decibel audit of your life. Notice the various ways you are assaulted on a daily basis by noise. Then, do something about it. Free yourself from the tyranny of a ringing telephone, for example. Many of the so-called time-saving and convenient appliances in our lives have somehow turned into demanding task masters. The telephone is like that for me. Even the ring of a telephone will cause my jaw to tighten, particularly when I am concentrating or relaxing.

Recently, I gave a keynote speech at a telecommunications conference. During my talk, I asked them this: "Why can't we invent a telephone system that notifies us of calls without making any noise?" After my talk, several executives told me that there is a device, used by people with hearing disorders, that attaches to your wrist and vibrates slightly when a call is for you. The only reason it isn't employed universally is simple; we have always had ringing telephones. It is the way "it is done."

I don't accept that reasoning anymore in my life. I can imagine a large cubical-filled office in which everyone has a device that notifies them silently when a call is for them. I believe the silence and peace generated by that one simple change would revolutionize our work environments.

Until this practice becomes common in our society, it will be up to you to create your own silence. You do not need to be a slave to your telephone, fax, or computer. We aren't Pavlovian dogs who must respond to a ringing bell. You may wish to turn off your telephone for a few hours each day so that you can complete paperwork—or sit in the sun. Get a good answering machine or voicemail system and let your friends know that you expect them to use it. Instruct your secretary and co-workers that when your door is closed it means you do not wish to be disturbed. Tell your family that your bath or quiet time is sacred.

Try driving with the radio off. Notice the color of the sky, the shape of the road, the look of the neighborhood. Practice turning off all mechanical interruptions for an hour each evening and spend the time in silence or quiet conversation. Listen to the birds outside the window, the wind in the trees, or your own breathing.

Search your home and work environment for sacred space. It doesn't need to be fancy unless you wish it to be. Creating a sanctuary does not mean becoming a hermit or building a walled security prison to keep the rest of the world out. What creating a sanctuary means is discovering ways to nurture yourself and your spirit wherever you may be. Create a place in your home, even if it is just a particular chair, where you go to be alone. Then make sure that everyone knows about it so you are not disturbed when using it.

In creating sacred space, it is important to remind yourself of your priorities and who you really are. The ways in which you do this will be very individual. For example, surrounding yourself with the things that you love will give you a sense of stability and groundedness. Many of us do this unconsciously by having photographs of loved ones on our desks and keeping mementos of pleasant times nearby. It is much more effective, however, if we do this consciously.

Creating an Altar

Many people enjoy creating altars to help remind them of what is important and what is sacred. If this appeals to you, find a place to create an altar or sanctuary and make it your own. Take a moment to think about items that bring you a feeling of peace and serenity. Examples are such things as flowers, rocks, photographs, and teddy bears. Think of things that are important to you and then try to think of a physical manifestation or representation of this thing. Christians use the cross to remind them of their faith. In the same way, you can use symbols to remind you of the things that are important to you.

Many people find that creating an altar in their homes and offices gives them a place to go to ground themselves and remember what is important. Find a place where you can gather items of personal significance to you and place them in a pattern you find pleasing. If having an altar appeals to you, feel free to incorporate it in to your intuitive practice. As a preparation for the intuitive exercises, you would go first to your altar. Pick up each item while taking a deep breath and let it remind you of its significance. Then place it in its correct place according to intuition. Do this with each item. Perhaps you might wish to use a short prayer stating that the best will come of this matter. This simple exercise can be done quickly and without anyone knowing what you are doing. If anyone asks, you can simply tell them that you are dusting or admiring your collection. There is no reason to explain the significance of your altar unless you trust the individual involved.

Once you have carved out your sacred time, silence, and space, you will use them for the intuitive practices discussed in the remainder of this book. Be aware that you need to be vigilant in protecting your right to time, privacy, and silence. Use this week to evaluate these things and make plans. What will you do if your children insist on speaking to you during your quiet times? How can you keep interruptions away? Preparing for these things, before they distract you, will be a large step toward obtaining the intuitive advantage.

3

crafting your questions

Many people are incredibly sloppy when they ask intuitive questions. When I do readings for people, I am always asked questions such as "Will I ever be happy?" or even "Am I going to die?" The answers to these questions, of course, is "yes"—even the most depressed among us experiences moments of happiness and, of course, we will all ultimately die. But those answers are not what the person truly wants to know. The true desire behind the question is, perhaps, something like "What can I do to improve my enjoyment of life right now?" or, "Do I currently have any health problems which could cause serious illness?"

Phrasing a proper question can take ten or more minutes, even when you think that you know very well what your question is all about. The question needs to be phrased specifically. "Will I marry Bill this year?" is a better question than "Will I ever get married?" The best questions are phrased in present-time terms. "What practices should I do now to improve my psychic ability?" rather than "Will I become a psychic?" The best questions, in my opinion, are those which ask for advice, rather than for prediction. "What can I do to improve my marriage?" as opposed to "Will I get divorced?"

While in one sense intuitive practices are games that sharpen your ability, in another sense they are very serious. For that reason, I advise people not to ask questions about which they know (or think they know) the answer. This sort of "testing" of the process is merely your conscious mind attempting to regain control. If you truly wish to have the intuitive advantage, you need to trust the process and not set yourself up.

This week you will practice crafting good intuitive questions. During the course of this program, you will be using these questions for various upcoming exercises. You can always change your questions or write new ones, but it good to have a "stock" of at least twenty questions to use when you need them.

Start by sitting quietly in your sacred space, put yourself in a focus state, and ask yourself, "What do I want or need to know?" Then, in your intuition notebook, record the questions that come to mind, making sure that you craft them to state what you truly want to know. Take your time, breathe, write your questions, and then forget them until needed.

It is important to remember that intuition is about knowing things, not creating things. Many people become confused about this because they are somewhat familiar with the concepts of creative visualization or manifestation.

Detachment vs. Visualization

Creative visualization is a popular and important technique used by many people. It is important to note here, however, that visualization is not intuition. When you visualize something, particularly an outcome or event, you are automatically making judgments about it. Many of us use visualization as a way to create new realities in our lives. For this purpose, it is an excellent tool. It is a very efficient technique for helping you to change your self-image and for eliminating faulty expectations. It is not inner knowing, however; it is inner programming. One of the defining characteristics of intuition is that it contains no judgments.

If you wish to be a proficient public speaker, for example, it is very helpful to visualize yourself going up to a podium and giving a flawless and confident speech. But do not deceive yourself into thinking that your intuition is telling you that this will happen. Your conscious mind is in charge of creating the visualization, and you have created strong judgments about the event. In this case, the judgment is that giving a speech with confidence is a good thing. The very use of these judgments will cloud your intuitive knowing of the event itself.

An organization with which I am affiliated recently sponsored a large event at a convention center. There was a great deal of money involved and it was a considerable risk for the event planners. After one planning meeting, one of the organizers called me and said, "My intuition is telling me that the room will be overflowing with people! I know this event is going to be highly successful. We all have been visualizing a packed auditorium."

This is an example of visualization, not intuition. My friend's investment in the event, both financial and emotional, made it almost impossible for her to be impartial about the outcome. In her mind, there was only one "good" outcome—one with a huge turnout. The committee's visualization of a large crowd may very well influence the attendance, but their strong desire and the very act of the visualization will taint their intuitive knowing about the attendance.

I am not, in any way, criticizing or negating visualization. I find it to be a tool that I use frequently. However, it is not intuition. If our desires are so strong that we want to use our intuition as a tool for creation of an outcome, we are likely to become very confused, and later, to blame our intuition for leading us astray.

Learning to avoid value judgments has been a difficult thing for me in my intuitive journey. I have learned through hard experience that the minute I judge an intuitive thought or feeling as "good" or "bad," "right" or "wrong," I lose my intuitive edge. Without any intention of doing so, value judgments color our knowing, causing us to lose the truth of the matter.

For example, you may have an intuitive flash that the company for which you work is having financial troubles. It will be tempting for you to label this as a "bad" thing, and to react in that fashion. Perhaps you decide to look for other work, or perhaps you become so depressed that your performance suffers. It is important to realize that your reaction will be based on your perception of the intuition and not the intuition itself. If you had not labeled this knowing as "bad," you might see it as an opportunity. It might prod you to share a profitable idea with a superior that could improve the company's, and your, future. Maybe it will prompt a re-evaluation of your lifestyle causing you to work fewer hours, dramatically improving your concentration and creativity, and perhaps even your marriage. The point here is that the judgment of a thing is seldom accurate until long after the event itself is over.

It is helpful for me to remember that my life is similar to an epic film whose content and quality is determined by when the film starts and ends. For example, if you made a movie of my life during the 1980's it would, in all likelihood, be classified as a tragedy, full of illness and addiction. Starting the film ten years later might turn it into an adventure story, and ten years earlier it could be a romance. As a life saga, it appears to be turning out as a comedy.

The important thing to remember is that any event in our lives can be interpreted in many different ways. Everyone has had instances in their lives that at the time seemed to be catastrophes, but, looking back a few years later, were re-interpreted as "the best thing that ever happened to me." For intuition purposes, you are given information without value judgments attached. It is your conscious mind that labels things "good" or "bad." Avoiding these judgments is a very important element in making intuition a useable tool for you.

As you work the exercises throughout this book, always remember to ask yourself this question, "Am I doing this out of a sense of detachment or is there an underlying judgment attached to my knowing?" If you feel any sense of investment or emotion in the outcome, you know you have not detached and that your intuition may be "tainted." This is not "bad," but it does mean that you may need to use another technique or enlist help from an intuitive friend in regard to that topic.

4

looking for signs

All around me, the surface on which I was standing was crystalline polished frozen lava. As it hardened, the lava had solidified into waves of ebony, many feet deep. Standing in the middle of a lava flow is like standing in the midst of a wasteland, beautiful yet barren. Looking in all directions, I could see nothing but black. And yet, as I looked closer, small bits of green were barely visible. In the midst of such devastation, plants were beginning to miraculously emerge. Once I opened my eyes to look for life, I could see it everywhere. To my right, I even saw a tiny flower blooming.

Volcano National Park on the big island of Hawaii is an awe-inspiring sight. An active volcano still rages, though its lava flow is now underground, visible only when it reaches the sea, causing steam to rise hundreds of feet into the air. Ancient flows of lava blend with the more recent ones creating a land of desolation and wonder. As I gazed at the tiny blossom emerging from the lava flow, I remembered a time in my own life when I had had a similar resurrection experience.

I had been in the intensive care unit of Fairview Hospital for over a month. The perforated esophagus had caused most of my internal organs to cease functioning, and I was kept alive by a catheter that pumped nutrients directly into a vein while six chest tubes pumped poisons out of my body. Too weak to sit up or move and unable to either eat or drink, I spent my days in a semi-trance, only barely aware of what was happening to me. One day, though, I noticed that as my legs rubbed together I could feel hair growing on them. I started to laugh, which alarmed the nurses so much that they came running to my bedside. "Look," I cried. "Nothing else in my body is working, but the hair on my legs is still growing!" I learned later that the nurses had written on my chart that I was delirious. But I was not. I was awe inspired by the persistence of life. I took the growth of hair as a sign of survival. From that moment, I knew I was going to live.

My family has always looked for signs. Sometimes my mother would take that to an extreme, seeing a dropped fork as a sign that I should do the dishes, for example. Still, I was taught not to take things at face value. At a young age I learned to ask, "What is this saying to me?" and it has been a valuable tool in my life.

This week you will also look for signs. For this assignment, you need to become aware of your environment. Look for things in your life that seem to be speaking to you. And then, most importantly, ask them what they have to say to you. You may be surprised by the answer. Don't try to figure it out or analyze your way through it. Just ask your intuition to tell you what a particular sign has to say to you, then write the answers in your intuition notebook.

Remember that the meaning of signs may be very different to different people. There is no one right or wrong answer. There is only your individual truth. I learned this a few years ago while on vacation with my family on Mexico's Yucatan peninsula. One day we left the beach to visit the ancient Mayan ruin of Coba. Unlike the more popular ruins of Chichen Itza and Tulum, Coba is largely unexcavated and, therefore, not heavily visited. We were among only a handful of tourists in the entire area. Narrow jungle roads separate the excavated sites. We headed toward one of the sites down a path at least a mile long, meeting no one along the way and hearing no sounds except the birds and other rustling jungle noises. Finally reaching the site, we spent about half an hour thoroughly exploring the ruins. Our group of five, my husband, my sister and her husband, and my brother rejoiced in having the area completely to ourselves.

Finally, we left to visit another site, returning on the same (and only) pathway. We walked slowly, looking for Toucans and admiring the large trees that surrounded us. Suddenly, a stranger who seemed to come out of nowhere joined us. Our new addition was indeed a strange person. He was tall and gangly and wore unusually colorful and baggy pants and a shirt with puffy sleeves. His clothes and demeanor made him look like a cross between a circus clown and a medieval troubadour. His wild red hair hadn't seen a comb for a long time. He joined our party, falling in step with my brother Jim, nodding and saying hello in a heavily accented voice. We were all shaken and uncomfortable. There had been no one else at the ruins we had just visited and no other way in or out except by this path. He seemed to have appeared out of thin air.

We walked together for a short time in what was now an awkward silence. None of us felt comfortable with our new friend, yet we weren't sure what to do. Finally, my sister and I stopped to admire a large spider web. Our friend stopped too. We waited. He waited. Then, perhaps sensing his lack of welcome, he left our group and walked on in front of us. As he walked away, we all noticed that he was carrying something in his right hand, but none of us could say what it was. He held it out admiringly in front of him as he walked. It seemed to be a cylindrical object of some kind, which glowed as the sun struck it. I thought I sensed energy waves emanating from it. Feeling freed, we followed him at a distance of less than 200 feet. At one point the path made a turn and we lost sight of him for a few minutes. When we made the turn, he had disappeared.

Then began the speculation about our visitor. My husband, as down-to-earth and logical as they come, declared him to be a German tourist with poor taste in clothes and a severe drug problem. He explained his sudden appearance by saying that he could have been asleep hidden in the ruins, and awakened after we left to follow us. Then he must have left the path at the turn to hide in the jungle or make his own path to another site. I declared, only half jokingly, that he was a visitor from space, materializing to join us for a few minutes and then using the magical device he held in his hand to transport himself elsewhere. Our group laughingly enjoyed the speculation as we walked to the next site.

The last ruin we saw at Coba was the pyramid. There we finally ran into a crowd, a busload of tourists stood photographing the structure. And, on a bench by himself, sat the man I had come to call Starman. He looked up at us and nodded. Speculation continued as we walked to the gate. How had he beaten us to the Pyramid without ever re-appearing on the path? Leaving him napping on the bench, we picked up our car in the parking lot and drove several miles down the road, stopping at a tiny town to have lunch. We sat at a table in an outdoor cafe. As we finished our meals, we were shocked to see Starman once again. He was walking down the highway toward Coba—coming from the opposite direction of where we had seen him last.

We had left him a half-hour before, sitting at a pyramid in a ruin at least three miles away. It was impossible for him to have walked that far in that amount of time, yet there was no sign of any companion or a vehicle. Even my logical husband was having a hard time coming up with an explanation, although hitchhiking was his final conclusion. But why, if he hitchhiked away from Coba, was he now walking toward it. And who gave him the ride? The tour bus?

I will never know, of course, who or what Starman was. I only know that the world is full of unexplained phenomena. People like my husband feel more comfortable with logical explanations, even when they have to stretch logic to an extreme. People like myself look for signs in everything, even when there might be a more logical explanation. Sometimes, the truth is very different for each person, even when experiencing the same event. I have learned that I only need to know what message an event or thing has for me, and then let others define their own truth in their own fashion. This week you will learn to do the same.

Looking for signs can be of great value when learning to use your intuition. Remember that intuition often speaks symbolically. Sometimes my students ask me, "What does this or that symbol mean?" But no one else can tell you what your signs mean. My story of the hospital is meant to remind you that the very sign that meant life to me was interpreted as a hallucination by the medical staff. The story of Coba tells you that different people can experience the same event and have drastically varied versions of its meaning.

It is up to you to interpret your own signs. If you experience an event or see something that has symbolic meaning to you, ask your intuition, "What does this mean?" Sit quietly and let the answer resonate in your soul, and then act on that knowing. I think you'll be surprised at how much better your life will be.

5

letting yourself go

"She's really let herself go," I heard my mother murmur in that stage whisper she used that could be heard around the block. I squirmed in the church pew to see what she meant. It was "Aunt" Agnes she was discussing. Agnes wasn't actually my aunt, but, since she was a childless "old maid," she had been adopted as my honorary auntie. I'm not sure either she or I appreciated that fact. I pondered the phrase "letting herself go" as the sermon droned on. What did it mean, I wondered? Agnes did wear funny clothes—big clunky "sensible" hiking shoes and unusual split skirts. Practical for hiking in the woods collecting flower samples, she'd told me. She didn't wear any makeup, refused to squeeze into a girdle, and pretty clearly had never spent a miserable night with her hair set in rollers. "Was that what my mother meant?" I wondered.

If so, I vowed that when I got old I'd let myself go also. A child of the 50's, I watched my mother wrestle her flesh into form-fitting girdles which only served to force the fat out over the top and under the knees. Even though I was, at that time, skinny as a rail, I got my first girdle when I turned twelve. It was hot and uncomfortable, and the tabs that held up my nylons bit into my legs. We set our hair each night on bristly rollers that ripped out more hair than they curled. I learned to tweeze my unruly eyebrows and curl the few eyelashes I had. Every part of my body needed to be controlled, it seemed. Becoming a woman meant a lifetime of monitoring body parts—too much here, too little there. All for the sake of being attractive and, of course, getting a man.

I believed that story. I was excited to get my first push-up bra, uncomfortable as it was. I got my straight fine hair permed, dyed, and curled. I lined my lips and eyes and colored my face. I wore shoes with three-inch heels that permanently damaged my toes. But I never forgot the promise I made to myself. "When I get old, I'm going to let myself go."

The problem with being a baby boomer is that no one seems to allow me to get old. The definition of "old" has changed. I suspect that we baby boomers will always define "old" as being five years older than we are—whatever that is. I know Aunt Agnes was considered to be old by the time she hit forty, perhaps even earlier. She became timeless, never changing her style, never really aging, staying at a perpetual "old" age.

Perhaps we don't have to get old to let ourselves go. Consider that fact that you could let yourself go right now. It is time to tire of holding the reins back. For myself, I'm dropping them and taking the risk that I won't go charging off a cliff like a team of horses longing to gallop after a lifetime of ladylike trotting.

So what does this have to do with intuition? Letting yourself go is one of the true keys to getting the intuitive advantage. In my opinion, one of the main things that stops people from using their intuition is the fear of looking foolish. For many years, I have been training business and professional people, as well as police and corrections officers in the use of intuition for their professions. In all of these training sessions, one of my biggest challenges is encouraging my students to drop their skepticism. Being a skeptic has become a source of pride for many in our society. But, in actuality it keeps them stuck. Some of my students are so afraid of looking gullible that they would rather not do anything at all. But all that accomplishes is keeping them from experiencing new ideas, from trying new techniques. It is guaranteed to squelch intuition. I always encourage my students to keep an open mind. I suggest to them, at least during the training, to put their skepticism in their pockets. Then, when they are done with the program, they will certainly be able to find it and use it again if it serves a purpose.

Developing an open mind goes beyond merely being willing to consider new ideas or exposing yourself to fresh teachings. Picture what it would look like to truly possess an open mind. When I visualize an open mind, I see a brain into which ideas and concepts flow like water into a glass. Is your mind able to hold all of this new material or is it too full of old concerns, resentments, and regrets? This is where letting go comes in. In order for new things and ideas to come into your life, you need to have space for them.

Being open-minded necessitates being in a state of "not fullness." It may not be necessary or even best to be in a state of emptiness, but it is crucial that there is space in your mind for new thoughts and ideas to grow and be nurtured. It not only means that you need to consider new things, it also means that you must let go of the old.

This week, your assignment is to consider what things you can let go of from your life in order to have room for intuitive ideas to fit. Perhaps you need to let go of ideas, attachment to certain ways of living, or ways of viewing yourself. Or, maybe you need to let go of actual physical objects, people, or commitments that take time that you no longer want to give.

In my life, I have discovered that giving away, selling, or discarding things I no longer need is incredibly freeing. You may wish to start by evaluating your lifestyle and asking about each possession: "Does this thing match my values and my favored lifestyle? Does it truly bring me satisfaction and joy? Do I use it? How much does it cost for me to own this-both financially and emotionally? How much time do I spend caring for, cleaning, and worrying about it? Do I insure it, store it, or provide security for it? Would I miss it if it were gone?"

There is no one thing or category of possessions that is inherently extraneous. Each person must make their own decisions based on their own values and lifestyle. It is virtually certain, however, that you are drowning in unused possessions. A good rule of thumb is that if you haven't used or worn something for over a year, you should get rid of it. Go through your home and workplace with new, more intuitive eyes. Then ruthlessly throw out or give away any item that you don't need or which does not provide you with a sense of sanctuary. After this cleansing, ask yourself how you feel. If you miss some of your items, you can be sure that you will soon accumulate more. If you feel a new sense of freedom and serenity, then you need to be on constant guard against encroaching possessions that will interpose themselves back into your space, mind, and heart.

Letting go of the grasp that material objects have upon you will give you a sense of exhilaration. But even more freeing is letting go of relationships that you have outgrown or are interfering with your life. In order to do this, you need to evaluate all of your relationships to determine which of them provide you with peace and serenity. Many of us have friends, family members, and even lovers who only cause us to feel angry and stressed. Often we have been involved with these people for so long that we continue the relationship out of habit.

Now is a good time to look at your associations and how you spend your time. This week make a note of who you see socially, at work, in your family, and in organizations. Jot down where you go and whom you see. Notice who you talk to on the telephone and the length of the call. Then rate each of these contacts based on the feelings that they generate within your deepest and most intuitive knowing. Which of your contacts made you feel upbeat and peaceful? Which of them increased your stress level? Which one of these people will support you in your quest for the intuitive advantage? Which of your acquaintances will belittle your efforts? Do you really want or need to spend time with people who cannot or will not understand your desire to improve your life?

We often grow or change so much that our old friends no longer fit in our lives. When that happens, we must develop the courage to say goodbye and wish them the highest possible good. It is probable that they are dissatisfied with the relationship also but have not yet figured out a way to end it. Do not let yourself be trapped in a cycle where you are forced to spend time with people who do not share your journey. Feelings and emotions are very powerful and spread easily. Negativity and depression are infectious. It is very difficult to be intuitive when you spend time with people who make fun of your efforts and undermine your determination.

Make sure that you evaluate the groups and organizations to which you belong. While pursuing your intuitive ability, it is helpful to surround yourself with people and things that nurture and support you. Ask yourself these questions: "Does this organization provide me with supportive friends and a nurturing environment? Will it encourage me to be myself, to let go of anything that is holding me back and support my intuitive ability?" If not, this is a good week to look for new supportive friends, organizations, and support groups. Take the time to attend different churches, groups, and classes that will support you in your efforts. In a later chapter, we will discuss forming intuitive communities. But even now, you should keep your eyes open for places that feed your soul.

You may also wish to use this week to re-evaluate your hobbies and interests. It may be that you are continuing a hobby only because someone gave you the tools or equipment. Maybe you do things because you used to enjoy it but you've long since lost interest, or maybe you attend concerts or plays only because a friend or family member enjoys them. Letting yourself go involves learning what you enjoy doing for recreation and doing as much of that as possible. It also means not doing things you don't enjoy, even if everyone else in your life thinks that you should.

My husband is an avid golfer. For Christmas a few years ago he gave me a set of clubs and has been adding to my golf equipment ever since. I took lessons and made an effort to learn to love the sport the way he does. For years we spent many hours on the golf course. I enjoyed the companionship and watching his joy. I appreciated the beauty of the natural setting. But finally, in my soul, I had to admit, I just don't like to golf.

What I was doing was giving up my choice of activities to spend time doing what my husband loves. This is encouraged in our society, but does it make sense? As I started evaluating my own life, I needed to look at all the superfluous activities in which I was involved. In order to find time for my own spiritual and intuitive quest, I needed to give up all the things I didn't passionately love. Golf lost. This doesn't mean I can't and won't spend time with my husband. Spending time with him is one of the things I love. I let go of an activity, not a person.

Take time this week to let go of things you no longer need or enjoy so that you have space for your intuition to blossom. Space to grow, learn, and develop new skills. Space to become yourself. Don't think of it as losing something; think of it as clearing the way for the new. Letting go—of ideas, things, relationships, groups, or hobbies, can be extremely freeing. And freedom is one of the true gifts of the intuitive advantage.

6

listening to nature

Nature speaks to us intuitively. At one time or another, most of us have felt the need to lie under a tree or take a walk to "clear our mind." Intuitively, we are drawn to the out-of-doors as a source of wisdom. We know that we can get answers to some of life's hardest questions by talking to nature. As children we may have had the experience of actually talking to a nature sprite or fairy. As we get older, our conscious mind won't accept such "fantasy," but we can still ask questions of nature and be confident that we will receive answers.

This week, your assignment is to spend as much time as possible out-of-doors. If you, like I, live in a cold weather climate and are reading this in the winter, you may need to compromise by going to a conservatory or greenhouse. Still, except in the most inclement conditions, you can always take a walk. Those of you in large cities may need to seek out parks, while others may only need to rest in their yards. The setting is not as relevant as the intent. Go to a place with natural life, and ask it questions.

You have created some questions in Chapter Three and have probably been wondering when you will use them. This will be the first of many opportunities to discover answers to these questions. Pick one of your questions, preferably without knowing which one it is, and put it in your pocket. Then take a seat in your yard, rest your back against a tree, or take a walk down a leafy street. Ask the universe to let nature answer your question, focus, and relax. In a short time, your attention will be drawn to an element of nature. Perhaps you will see a particularly beautiful tree or notice a squirrel run past you. Assume that you have just received an answer. Then, read your question, relax again and ask your intuition to explain the answer.

I did this exercise during a particularly stressful time in a relationship. A good friend and I had been having a series of arguments which were distressing both of us but which we didn't seem able to resolve. One of my questions was: "How can I better understand my relationship with my friend?" It was a cold November Minnesota day and I was reluctant to go outside. Still, I felt a need to take a walk and trusted my body enough to follow its urging. It was a chilly gray day and nature seemed far away. About all I saw were dirty slushy streets and dry lifeless trees. Then, suddenly a flock of huge crows seemed to come out of nowhere. They landed on the trees and sidewalks, cawing and complaining. Where there had been silence, there was a cacophony of noise. This was my answer, I was sure of it. But what did it mean?

When you want an interpretation of your intuitive knowing, you can enlist the help of your analytical brain. Crows, I thought, were social animals indicating a relationship issue. Their huge size illustrated the size this issue had come to have in my life. Still, I thought, they were actually having a good time, talking, and what, for a crow, I interpreted as laughing. Even in the dead of winter, the crows seemed joyful. What message was there for me? Well, lately my conversations with my friend had been anything but joyful. We had done a lot of talking, but not much laughing. The more I watched the crows, the less serious our arguments seemed to be. As I walked home I resolved to call my friend and have a playful and fun conversation.

You might have seen the same flock of crows and had a completely different interpretation. That is how intuition acts. Even though there are many books on the market telling you what symbols mean, my belief is that every one of us knows our own symbols. Claiming the intuitive advantage means finding your own interpretation to your intuitive knowledge, and then trusting it enough to act upon it.

The natural world is a huge teacher for us. Just as it gives us individual messages, it also gives us societal messages. I believe we are in a pivotal time of human history. We are standing on the precipice of a new millennium, uncertain as to what comes next. We need to use our intuition as a society to help us survive and thrive. Industrial society has always prided itself on controlling the natural world. But, perhaps, the third millennium will be the era of relinquishing control—or, to be truthful, the illusion of control. Since the dawn of the industrial revolution, people have nurtured the idea that we can control our destinies, our world, and our bodies. One of the lessons of the new millennium is that we are not in control. The recent flooding in the Midwest can be seen as a good example of this.

— Winter and spring of 1997 certainly had an apocalyptic flavor for the people in northwestern Minnesota and North Dakota. First, tremendous blizzards kept people throughout the region from venturing from their homes for weeks at a time. The snow and ice storms downed power lines, causing electrical outages that lasted for up to ten days. On the heels of the worst winter in anyone's memory came the floods of '97. After weeks of frantic sandbagging, often during snowstorms and freezing cold, the dikes burst and entire cities were flooded. East Grand Forks, Minnesota, and Grand Forks, North Dakota, were evacuated, with thousands of refugees forced to live for weeks in emergency shelters. Up to 75% of both cities was destroyed.

There is perhaps no place in the United States where the people are more down-to-earth and practical than in that area of the country. These are farm families, raised to believe in self-sufficiency and hard work. They have experienced flooding before from the mighty Red River and they expect to see it again. Even so, the 1997 season left many shaking their heads in wonder. This was different than anything in memory. Could it be a sign of the beginning of the end? It was a 500-year flood, they were told. Of course, weather records don't tell the tale of catastrophic flooding, tornadoes, hurricanes, and the like 500 years ago. What would a flood of 1497 have looked like?

The Red River Valley is a dried lake bottom, created thousands of years ago by glaciers crossing the area. Because of this, the rivers have always flooded widely. Until towns and cities, farms, and factories were built along the riverbanks, flooding was of little consequence. When the waters rose, life along the river moved to drier quarters, leaving behind nothing that could not be easily re-built. The flooded land would soon dry out, the only lasting effect being an increase in fertility caused by silt deposited by the floodwaters. A flood of the magnitude of 1997 occurring in 1497 would just be a flood, not a disaster.

One prediction you can count on as we begin the new millennium is that severe and apocalyptic weather patterns will become the norm. We will experience billions of dollars in property loss. Insurance companies will find it harder and harder to pay claims and all of our insurance rates will soar. The federal disaster funds will be taxed to the limit, as will the funds available to the Red Cross, Salvation Army, and other relief associations. The wonderful outpouring of giving seen after the Red River flooding showed a gracious and generous spirit of neighborliness. But will it continue for the next disaster, and the one after that?

Why will we continue to see so many natural "disasters?"

Because there are so many people. It was the building of permanent structures in the Red River Valley that caused the floods to become a problem. As people continue to spread throughout the world, we build homes, businesses, and towns in areas that are highly subject to nature's wrath. We are building million-dollar homes in flood plains and on the sides of mountains that are subject to mudslides. We erect massive settlements on fragile eco-systems.

The more people affected, the greater we define the disaster. So, of course, we can with certainty predict that greater and greater disasters will occur. About one hundred years ago, a comet hit in a nearly unsettled area of Russia, creating a crater a mile wide. Because the area was virtually empty, very little actual damage was caused. Imagine however, the disaster that a similar comet landing would cause if it landed today in a major metropolitan area. We would have a death toll in the millions and property destruction in the billions. The insurance industry would collapse, causing massive worldwide economic difficulty. Everyone in the world would be affected by an event that, one hundred years ago, barely made headlines.

The Chinese language uses the same character for the word "opportunity" as it does for the word "crisis." I believe that western society must also begin to look at crises not just as a challenge to be overcome but as messages that need to be heard. Crises such as the floods in the Red River Valley could be used to prompt city, state, and federal leadership to use the opportunity to look at a whole new way to rebuild these cities.

With so much of the region destroyed, entire new ways of building cities could be considered. Perhaps, instead of single family homes, each on their own one-acre plot, cluster homes could be built. Green areas that could handle the floods each spring could be built. Residents and non-residents alike could take time to evaluate their lives, their possessions, and what they really need and want. Perhaps, instead of replacing everyone's individual snowblower, lawnmower, ladder, and power tools, a neighborhood tool center could be built where only one such item would be necessary per block.

We have come to a time where we need to listen to nature, both in our individual lives and in our society. How do we wish to live as human beings? What can we control, and what can we not? What do we let go of? It is time for all of us as a society to examine how we live and what we value—before the next disaster strikes.

Use this week to ponder the lessons that nature is teaching you. Get out in nature, hug a tree, take a walk, and ask nature to give you messages. You will be surprised at what you learn.

7

talk to your body

During every waking second, we are bombarded by visual, auditory, and sensory data—not to mention the information we receive through our intuition. We learn very quickly to filter most of this material out and to focus on only a very small amount of the information that we are receiving. If we were unable to do so, we would probably be unable to function in our world.

Take a moment and attempt to fully concentrate on all the information you are receiving from your senses at this very moment. First, listen and attempt to identify all the sounds you hear. Right now, I am hearing the hum of my computer, a bird outside my window, a car driving by, the radio playing softly in another room, a rattle coming from my refrigerator, the sound of my breathing, the sound of my heartbeat, and much more. I am in a relatively quiet environment all by myself—imagine the multitude of sounds that we hear while in a busy store or office.

Now focus on the smells around you. I can smell the sharp scent of coffee from the cup nearby, but I also smell a faint tinge of mold, and an earthy smell I can't quite identify is emanating from my open window. I can also smell a faint perfume from the soap and shampoo of my morning shower.

My physical body is giving me many messages. I realize now that both of my wrists are aching slightly—a legacy from two broken wrists and too much typing. I feel the pressure of the chair on my bottom and thighs, the weight of eyeglasses on my nose, and an itch in one eye. The taste of coffee as I take a sip from the cup on my desk provides me with comforting warmth in my esophagus and a familiar, slightly acid flavor on my tongue.

Focusing on the visual images surrounding me is overwhelming. There are literally thousands of items within the range of my vision. The screen of my computer contains hundreds of different letters, icons, and colors. My small studio is filled with objects calling for my attention. With all of this information constantly available, how do I know which to concentrate upon? And, even more importantly, how do I recognize an intuitive signal if it is trying to capture my attention amid this cacophony of sensory input?

This week's lesson will be about using the information

that your body is receiving and giving to you. Your primary intuitive focus this week will be to monitor your body. Notice the messages it is giving you and then ask these messages what they mean.

Many years ago, while recovering from numerous surgeries, I developed a morning ritual, which I use to this day. At that time, I was in a great deal of pain. I had endured two chest surgeries and a number of smaller medical procedures that had ravaged my body. The pain was so intense that there were days that it seemed to require most of my focus.

Mostly by accident (although also, I now know, by intuition) I discovered that the pain was much more manageable if I could identify it as to its source and location. If I didn't do that, I discovered that the pain became a dictator of my entire being. Once I had located it and given it some attention, it stayed in the background and allowed me to focus on the rest of my life. So, every morning before I got out of bed, I would run a diagnostic on my body. I would start with my toes. "Any pain in my feet?" I would ask myself. I would move up through my legs, torso, stomach, chest, head, and so forth, checking out my body for pain. Once I located the pain, I would give it some attention to honor it and then would ask it to stay quiet unless there was some particular reason for me to know about it.

A strange ritual, I admit, but it became a valuable tool in my recovery. Even though I thought my entire body was wracked in pain, this diagnostic would demonstrate that the pain was generally only located in my chest cavity and stomach. Most of my body was pain free! This knowledge helped me to put pain in a proper perspective.

Nearly twenty years later, I still run my morning diagnostic. I am no longer in any type of acute pain, but I always find little aches and discomforts. Nowadays, I have learned to use this information for intuitive purposes. When I find a discomfort, I speak to it. For example, the last week or so I have often awakened with a slight headache. Speaking to the headache, I asked what it had to tell me. Recently it told me that it needs less caffeine, particularly at night. Other times, I might have an ache that will tell me it is due to grief, or even that it is in sympathy for someone else's pain.

Your body speaks to you all the time, in the only way it knows how. It gives you headaches, a sore neck, or gas. Most of us ignore these messages, maybe even taking a pill to make them go away. This week, instead of medicating your feelings, talk to them instead. For example, notice every time you get goosebumps. They are often a very strong intuitive message from your body. I consistently get them when I hear a strong and powerful truth. This might be a truth that is spoken to me by someone else, or one I read, or even one that comes from my own inner knowing. This has been so consistent for me that I have learned to trust it and act on it. My goosebumps are rarely wrong.

You might get goosebumps with a completely different message. Perhaps you get them when presented with a dangerous or risky situation, or when you are cold or lonely. The only way you can know what this bodily message means is to have a dialogue with it. Ask your body, "What does this reaction mean?" You will receive an answer. Don't doubt it or question it at this time. Merely record the instance, the bodily reaction and the interpretation in your intuition notebook.

For the next week, pay attention to the signals you are receiving from your body. Talk to them. Question them, and then record what you learn in your notebook. See if you find a pattern. I believe that you will find some very interesting and, perhaps, surprising things about the way your physical body speaks to you. One of my students did this exercise and told me that she discovered that she always got a slight pain in her back whenever a certain co-worker came into her office. When she questioned her intuition about this reaction, she heard that this person was "stabbing her in the back." Although she had no reason to believe this, she did decide to check out this intuitive message. As she subtly asked around the office, she discovered that this co-worker was, indeed, spreading false rumors about her. Based on this information, she was able to deal with the situation before it turned into a much worse problem.

Your body is very wise. Trust its messages to you. Honor its wisdom. Talk to it and it will talk back to you.

8

intuition and emotions

A prospective divorce client sat across the desk from me. She told a familiar enough tale, an emotionally abusive husband, two children, and a dead-end job. It seemed to be straightforward enough. We discussed the usual things, custody, maintenance, property settlement, and fees. Using the analytical skills that had been pounded into me in law school, I decided to take her case. Yet, the longer I spoke with her, the more uncomfortable I became. After she left my office I noticed that I was feeling anxious and fearful. I felt a need to light a candle, as if to cleanse the room in some matter. I quickly dismissed these sensations. I had a new case to work on and a sizable retainer check to deposit. All the facts were as they should be.

Over the next few weeks, my emotional response to my client became stronger and stronger. I couldn't call her without experiencing a sense of dread. My anxiety levels reached new heights whenever she came into my office. I was baffled by this emotional reaction. While I did not particularly enjoy practicing divorce law, it was, at that time, a large part of my practice. This case seemed common enough that there was no logical reason for my fear. Finally, I could no longer ignore my emotional reactions to her. I met with my client and requested that she hire a different attorney to take her case. For months I felt slightly guilty about this. Despite the fact that I had refunded her retainer and made the transition as easy for her as possible, I felt I had let her down. But mostly, I judged myself for being too emotional, too "weak" to be a good attorney.

Months later, I ran into her new attorney at the Courthouse. The custody study had just been completed, he told me, highlighting my former client's history of abusive behavior and mental illness. The "facts" she had given both of us about her case turned out to be primarily untrue. My logical assessment of the merits of her case had been based on her fictional account of her marriage. But my emotional response to my client had been 100 percent accurate.

Our society encourages us to rely on facts and logic and to ignore our emotions. But most of us know that our "gut feelings" tell us things that we don't always get from the so-called facts. Emotional reactions are just another way that our intuition speaks to us. This week we will be paying attention to these emotional reactions and watching them for intuitive messages.

Intuition tends to speak to us in five primary ways. Most commonly we merely have a thought—intuition frequently uses our thoughts as a way of communicating with us. As we will see in later chapters, intuition also speaks to us visually and, sometimes, even audibly. We see pictures in our mind's-eye or hear a voice in our head that seems to come from somewhere other than ourselves. Sometimes intuition gives us physical messages—a pain in the neck or stomach, goose-bumps, or tension. And often, intuition speaks to us through our emotions. We have, as the story above illustrates, an emotional reaction that may seem out of context but later proves to be accurate.

This week your assignment will be to practice listening to your intuitive emotions, distinguishing them from nonintuitive emotions and then acting on this intuitive knowledge. To begin with, spend a day or two simply monitoring your emotions. To do this, you may wish to carry your intuition notebook with you to note your reactions. People are emotional beings and experience feelings constantly. You first need to simply watch your emotions and identify them. It is an interesting experience to consciously label your emotions. You may even find that you are uncertain as to which emotion you are feeling. If so, don't anguish over this, just label it to the best of your ability.

As you go through your day labeling your emotions, notice when they seem to be elicited by the situation at hand

and when they appear to be inappropriate to the context. For example, if you feel angry or impatient because you are running late and your six-year-old has just spilled her milk, this emotion is appropriately linked to your situation and environment. If you feel this same emotion while making love to your husband, it may be an intuitive emotion with a message.

If you monitor your emotions, you will discover that they are often not traceable to what is happening to you at the time. You may find yourself feeling great sadness or joy "for no reason." Perhaps you are checking out at the grocery store when you feel a strong sense of grief. This emotion, unless directly linked with something that has happened, is intuitive. If this happens to you, jot down in your notebook what the emotion was and describe the circumstances you were in at the time. Don't analyze the meaning for now, just note the emotion. However, if you feel that you do understand the reason for this emotion or have an intuitive hit as to what it was telling you, feel free to record that as well.

For the first two days, though, your job is just to notice your emotions and distinguish between the ones which are prompted by outer circumstances and the emotions which seem to appear unrelated to what is happening around you. In general, it is this latter category of emotions that are giving you intuitive messages.

After a few days, you should be quite good at distinguishing between a so-called regular emotion and an intuitive emotion. Now, whenever you feel an intuitive emotion, add another step. Ask this emotion, "What are you trying to tell me?" Usually, you will get a very strong answer. If you don't, ask yourself this, "If I was getting a message from my emotions, what would it be?" Don't let your conscious logical mind talk you out of speaking to your emotions. If you speak nicely to them, they are happy to respond.

The last step in this week's journey into emotional intuition is to learn to be able to use this information. Remember that the intuitive advantage comes when you not only get intuition in an unsolicited fashion, but when you can control and use your intuition. Take at least one day (perhaps a weekend if that feels less vulnerable to you) and decide that you will ask your emotions for advice before making decisions. Then be brave enough to act on that advice.

Recently, I was taped for a television program featuring women intuitives. I was rather nervous about this and wanted to make sure that I looked and felt confident. None of the clothes in my closet seemed appropriate and I spent a frustrating day at the mall attempting to find a few outfits to wear for the filming.

The next day I decided to try again, this time by letting my intuition show me what was right for me. As I tried on outfits, I would ask my intuition, "How will I feel if I wear this?" It was fascinating for me to see how my emotions would give me messages. One suit, which my logical brain told me was perfect, made me feel extremely nervous. Another which looked great on me, elicited feelings of vulnerability. Finally, I slipped on a suit and immediately felt confident and calm. I bought it and felt those same emotions on the day of the taping.

Did I create all of those feelings in my mind? Was the confidence a self-fulfilling prophecy? The practical part of me doesn't care. I use intuition to aid my life and I have one measurement. If it improves my life, I keep doing it. If it doesn't, I stop.

Use the last few days of this week to ask your emotions about work, children, money, and purchasing issues. Then have the courage to act on what they tell you. And if life goes just a little bit better this week, keep doing it.

9

asking for messages

I was sitting cross-legged on red dirt, surrounded by six other people in similar poses. Even though it was pitch black, I could sense their presence, almost feel their emotions. The rocks in front of us had been heated until they glowed red and the smell of sage tinged the air with a slightly acrid scent. As Yellow Bird sang and prayed, he occasionally sprinkled water on the stones, creating a moist heat that caused perspiration to pour from my body.

It was my first time in a sweat lodge and I hadn't been sure what to expect. Would I be able to tolerate the heat and utter darkness? Could I really sit still for two-and-a-half hours? Would I have visions—or would I get bored? I had heard so many stories about sweat lodge transformations that I was both excited and apprehensive.

The sweat lodge experience consisted of four rounds of prayer and song. After each round more hot rocks were brought into the lodge. As the heat increased, I entered into a state of blissful unawareness. My body may have been seated on the moist red earth but my spirit soared high above. Silently, I asked the universe to give me a message. Almost immediately, I was enveloped in a bubble of calmness out of which came a gentle knowing. "Right now," I heard an inner voice say, "is the time of awakening. You are in the midst of an evolutionary change of epic proportions."

After the lodge was over, a shower taken, and dinner eaten, I sat and contemplated my inner message. "What," I wondered, "had I really heard?" My intuition answered me. "We are in the middle of a new renaissance, an age of inner enlightenment, an intuitive evolution. And, everyone has a job to do to bring it to fruition. Your role in this renaissance will be revealed to you if you just listen." I was told very clearly that it was important for me to ask for messages, and that I could be assured that I would receive them. I was also told that I would teach others to listen for these messages in their own lives. Part of the reason for my writing this book was because of the inner knowing I received that night.

Whether you ask for messages from Spirit, the Universe, or your inner self, you will get them—if you take the time to listen. You don't need to be in a sweat lodge or on a retreat in order to get messages. These experiences are helpful, though, because they encourage you to take time away from your daily routine, slow down your mind, focus, and, of course, listen. When I talk about receiving messages, many people look at me strangely. In the prevailing wisdom of our society, getting messages from an unseen force is tantamount with mental illness. Either you are seriously crazy or you are a mystic or psychic. In any event, most people don't believe that they can receive messages whenever they wish.

In order to truly have the intuitive advantage, you must first believe that messages are constantly available to you. Then you must learn to ask for these messages, listen to the answers, trust their wisdom, and act on their advice.

As obvious as it may appear, most people don't get messages because they don't ask for them. Think of your intuition as a giant voice mail system. It may be packed with messages, but unless you pick up the telephone and plug in the correct code, you won't receive them. This week, therefore, you will practice asking for and receiving messages on a daily basis. You will use a simple technique that I have found to be very useful in my life. For this technique to work, you need to be willing to play. Don't take yourself too seriously; just resolve to do the exercise for one week. If, at the end of the week, you have not enjoyed it or did not get receive anything from it, you can forget it and move on to other intuitive methods. As we have discussed before, no intuitive method works for everyone and no intuitive method works every time. You need to practice and experiment to find your own best methods and techniques.

Set aside about ten minutes a day to do this exercise. It is useful to do it at different times of the day in different settings. Sit quietly for a moment, holding one of the questions that you prepared earlier, or simply thinking of a question or issue in your life for which you would like guidance. Relax your tongue, or use some other focus technique to put you into a slight trance. Then, open your eyes, look around your environment and ask yourself three questions.

First, what thing in my line of vision attracts my attention? Second, what thing bothers or annoys me? And finally, what thing in this room or area has a message for me? Find these items as quickly as possible without any analysis of why they attract or repel you. Don't try to interpret their meaning, just note the items, perhaps jotting them down in your intuition notebook.

Take a few more moments of quiet meditative time; then, keeping your question in mind, interpret the meaning of your message. The item that attracted you symbolizes the question. Take a moment to ask yourself, "What does this item have to tell me about the nature of my question?" The item that annoyed you represents a warning or negative answer to the question, while the item with the message will give you advice on how to resolve your question.

As an example of how this exercise works, I used it this morning, asking, "What chapter of my book should I work on today?" I sat quietly at my kitchen table, loosened my tongue, and repeated this question silently to myself. When I opened my eyes, the first item I saw was my telephone. I wrote this down as the item that attracted my attention. Looking around the room, I noticed dirty dishes on the counter. It wasn't hard to figure out what annoyed me—especially since they had been left there by my husband. Finally, I was drawn to look out the window, just in time to see a Bluejay at my bird feeder. I asked him silently for a message.

Now, after gathering these three items, the fun began. Interpretation of intuitive messages is sometimes the most difficult task for people because they are afraid of being wrong. But, the great part about intuition is that you can't be wrong. Intuition is your personal legacy. No one else can truly interpret it for you (although it is nice to get help sometimes) and any meaning it has for you is the correct interpretation. In fact, when my students are blocked by their fear and insist that they "aren't getting anything," I tell them to "make something up." They are usually aghast at this suggestion, but it is valid. Intuition and imagination are sisters. All of this information comes from you—your brain—your inner knowing. You can't get it wrong!

When I asked my intuition for help in interpreting these messages, I was told that the telephone symbolized my desire to communicate clearly. The dirty dishes were a sign of interference and told me I was letting other things and people get in the way of my writing. And the Bluejay? Nature of course. I was told clearly to get out of my kitchen, without loading the dishwasher, go to my studio, and start my chapter on listening to nature.

10

using a pendulum

One of easiest to use, but in my opinion least reliable, tools of intuition is the use of a pendulum. I teach its use to my classes early in their training because, as with the use of dowsing rods, the use of a pendulum gives people something they can actually see and feel. When you use a pendulum, you have a visible sign that something is happening over which you have no conscious control. This makes it a powerful intuitive technique, although as we shall see later in this chapter, it also has some pitfalls.

A pendulum is a very simple device. All it consists of is a weight at the end of a string or chain. You undoubtedly have many things in your house that you can use to create pendulums. Any object on a chain, such as a pendant or necklace, can be used as a pendulum. Or, you can make a simple pendulum by tying a washer on a piece of string. Anything that will swing freely while you hold one end qualifies as a pendulum.

Eventually, if you like using this technique, you will most likely want to buy a professional pendulum. These are readily available in most metaphysical bookstores and catalogues. While you don't need anything fancy, there are some beautiful stones on silver or gold toned chains that many people find resonate better for them. The basic rule here is to use what is comfortable and works for you.

Once you have found a pendulum that swings freely, use it by holding the chain or string between your thumb and middle or index finger. Some people will tell you it is best to use one hand or the other or that you have to use certain fingers to hold the pendulum. Do what is most comfortable for you. It is usually easiest for me to rest my elbow on a flat surface, while holding the pendulum between my thumb and index finger. I also personally like to use a pendulum on a fairly short (3 to 4 inches) chain. You will need to experiment until you find the pendulum size, length of chain, and position that feel comfortable.

Once you are holding the pendulum comfortably and loosely, use your pendulum to give you an answer to which yes or no is the appropriate response. First, you must determine what yes and no look like using this particular pendulum. This will vary from person to person and pendulum to pendulum. Hold your pendulum loosely and ask it to show you "yes." It may take a little time, but eventually the stone or weight will begin to swing. Note the direction of the swing, then stop the pendulum and, when it is at rest, ask it to show you "no." There should be a noticeable difference in the way that the pendulum swings.

Once you have taken a "baseline" of your pendulum, you can ask it simple questions to which yes and no answers apply. It also can be used as a dowsing instrument for measuring energy flow. We will discuss this use in another chapter. Personally, I believe that the use of the pendulum is most valuable as a dowsing or energy reader and less valuable for prediction. However, many people like to use the pendulum to help them get started in making decisions. I know people who carry it with them to the store to help with purchasing decisions and to the library to find the best book to read. One client of mine even takes it to the casino to pick the best slot machine!

Remember though, that your emotions and desires are powerful and can unintentionally affect the messages that you get from all intuitive techniques. Because the pendulum is so sensitive to energy, it is particularly vulnerable to this. The following story illustrates how you must beware of "forcing" intuitive techniques to give you the answer you desire. If you find yourself asking the same question over and over again until you get the answer you want, you are no longer using intuition, you are using will.

Denise was angry. She had taken several of my intuition classes and had learned many techniques, which she practiced frequently. She came in for a private reading with me and made a demand. "I know Jonathan is going to die soon," she told me, "are you sure you don't see something about that?" I had to admit to her that I didn't. Still, I told her, I was doing a reading for her, not for Jonathan. "What is it that makes you so certain that your husband, a young and apparently healthy man, will soon die?" "I've used the pendulum dozens of time, asking that very question," she told me. "It always says he's going to die." Recently, as a matter of fact, it had even given her a date, although she admitted that she had also been certain he would die on other dates in the past. Despite this, Jonathan remained very much alive. "But, even if the date isn't true," she stated, "my intuition is so strong on this that I know I'm right!"

Denise's deep blue eyes filled with tears. She was an attractive, bright woman who had left a promising job to raise a family and dedicate herself to creating a beautiful home and supporting Jonathan's career. Now, she felt unfulfilled and lonely. She was unhappy in her marriage, feeling trapped and unsatisfied, but also believing that she couldn't leave. Her career skills were outdated and finances such that she'd have a difficult time making it on her own. She admitted that both she and Jonathan were good loving parents and she refused to submit their two small children to a custody battle. Although she would never admit it, Jonathan's death would solve some of these dilemmas. When I suggested that she might be confusing intuition with willfulness Denise became furious. "I don't know how you could suggest that!" she exploded. "I love Jonathan and would never want anything to happen to him—I just know it's going to, that's all."

The last time I saw Denise the so-called date for Jonathan's death had come and gone and they were still struggling in a troubled marriage. In my opinion, Denise's reliance on her "message" from the pendulum was only contributing to keeping her in a stuck situation. By placing false reliance on her "intuition" she could avoid the real work of finding a genuine solution to her marital and financial problems. I am not suggesting that she truly wanted or desired his death, only that she was engaged in "magical thinking" that suggested a force outside herself would take care of her marital issues without her direct intervention. Intuition does not solve your problems for you. It does help you to see what they are and provides you with new and innovative ways of looking at the issues.

Does this mean that intuition doesn't work? Of course not. This story does demonstrate the danger of expectation and desire of a particular outcome, however. One of the most vexing problems most of us face when attempting intuitive techniques is the issue of detachment. It is a well-known fact that it is difficult, if not impossible, to do a good "reading" on oneself. The reason? Our egos, fears, dreams, and wishes all get in the way of a true intuitive knowing. Despite this, all of us want to know more about what is going to happen to us and to understand more about ourselves. Is it impossible to truly use intuition for our own purposes?

No, but in order to do so, we must master one of life's true challenges—detachment and lack of judgment. True intuitive knowing can be best distinguished from a wish or fear by its lack of feeling. Intuition comes without underlying emotion. At best, true intuition appears as a neutral, impartial thought, picture, or knowing.

Often, these thoughts appear unbeckoned. You are driving down a road one morning when you suddenly see, in your mind's eye, your mother's face, then you think of the word California. These images appear without feeling and mean nothing to you. Probably you forget all about the incident until later that day when your mother calls to tell you of her trip plans—to California.

Contrast that incident to one in which you attempt to psychically determine the best move for your mother. Perhaps you are worried about her being alone and wish that she would travel more. Or, maybe you think she's spending too much money and think she should stay home. In this case, it is more than likely that any intuitive practices you use will be colored by your fears and wishes. A strong desire or dread will often cause you to believe that you are getting an intuitive thought, when, in fact, your conscious mind is making its case for or against something.

Our conscious logical mind uses just a minute portion of our total brain's functioning. Despite this, the conscious mind and its ego speak very loudly, and our intuition, even though stronger in power, is much softer in volume. Because of this, we sometimes have to "trick" the conscious into shutting up.

This is particularly true when we want information about things in which we have an emotional investment—such as relationships, finances, and work. That is the reason that so many of the intuitive techniques in this book may seem like tricks to you. In a way they are. You are trying to fool your conscious mind into staying out of the picture long enough to let your intuition do its work.

Does all of this mean you shouldn't try to use a pendulum? Absolutely not. It can be a valuable tool, and a lot of fun. Just don't attach yourself so much to a particular outcome that you allow yourself to sway (literally in this case) the answer you are receiving. This week's assignment is therefore particularly difficult. You not only will learn to use a pendulum, you will also practice detachment.

Start by asking the pendulum questions about which you have no emotional involvement. Ask for advice on issues about which you care very little. Or, ask for advice for other people. Be creative. Ask about which supplements would be helpful for you to take. Ask about what dog food is best for your pet. See if your plants need watering. Trust these answers, and be a little wary about inquiring into the state of your marriage. You are still a novice intuitive. Give yourself time to learn detachment—and practice, practice, practice.

This week, use a pendulum every day to make a decision about a non-emotional issue. Notice how it feels, experience the sense of detachment. Then, act on this knowing and note how successful it was for you in your intuition notebook.

11

intuition in the palm
of your hand

The Enchanted Garden Resort in Ocho Rios, Jamaica, is a truly magical place. Waterfalls cascade down the mountainside, interspersed with swimming pools and gorgeous gardens. I had been invited to spend a week there, giving lectures and reading palms; and I was feeling very blessed to have the sort of job that allowed me to work in such splendor. Somewhat ethnocentrically, I had assumed that my clientele would be largely the American and European resort guests. I was pleased and surprised to discover that most of my palmistry appointments were with the local people who had heard I was coming and called for consultations months in advance. It was fascinating to see the cultural differences that appeared on the hands of the Jamaican people. They are highly spiritual and independent and I felt honored to share in their lives, even in such a small fashion.

One of my appointments surprised me in many ways. He was a man in his late fifties, well dressed and soft spoken. He told me had come under duress upon his wife's insistence. It is always difficult to read the palm of one who doesn't wish to have it read. Still, after he relaxed and became comfortable with me, he was both open and fascinating. We took an immediate liking to each other. Almost as soon as I took his hand, we both felt an electric shock emanate from his middle finger. We jumped almost simultaneously, then looked at each other in surprise. As I moved my hand slowly over his hand without touching it, we both experienced the shock again. "What does that mean?" he asked.

"Your middle finger is your finger of leadership and service," I told him. "Combined with the strong fame line you have pointing to your little finger of communication, I am certain that you are writing a book which will influence the lives of others." As I told him this, I felt a strong intuitive knowing and heard in my mind information that seemed crucial for him to know. "You are writing a book right now, I think." I continued. "It feels as if you have strong ties with a government, although strangely enough, it doesn't appear to be Jamaican. I see you in a position of strong authority but also one that places you in great danger. You must finish this book, as it is very important. But, you also must be aware that the book will be only the start of your influence and leadership."

When I stopped speaking, I felt a little foolish. In truth, I hadn't seen any of this information on his palm; it had simply come from a strong intuitive knowing. But, it made no logical sense based on what little information I had about this man. I was certain he would laugh at me and it would verify for him that I was just another new-age kook his wife had dragged him to see.

He sat silently for awhile. Then he said soberly, "You couldn't possibly have known that until recently I held a very high position in a small South American country rather near here. I left suddenly when a change in the government almost certainly promised my imprisonment, or worse." He went on to tell me that he and his family had fled this country (which I do not feel free to name for the sake of his anonymity) and had come to Jamaica where he was a professor at a University in Kingston. They had traveled almost four hours to get this reading, because his wife, upon seeing my picture in the newspaper, had been certain he needed to talk to me. "I am writing a book," he continued, "about the economic policies of the Caribbean. If it is published, it will be very inflammatory." He also told me of his desire to return to his home country and enter into the political arena. His only concern was for the safety of his wife and children. Several years later, I can't tell you if the book has been published or if he has returned to the political scene. All I can tell you is this—that experience verified for me a very important lesson-a great deal can be learned by holding and feeling someone's hand, and it is important to have the courage to say what is seen.

I wrote my first book, *Your Life In the Palm of Your Hand,* so that I could teach my students the basic rules of palmistry. It remains a simple classic text for analysis of the hand. But, I also believe that there are times when the best thing to do is to throw away all the books and rules and use your intuition to read palms. This is the lesson that I wish you to practice this week.

As you probably know, all people have energy centers, called chakras, which line up along the spine of the body, extending both front and back. You may not know that you also have chakras on the soles of your feet and the palms of your hands. These energy centers vibrate with your energy and, when read intuitively, tell you a great deal about what is going on regarding yourself and others. When we felt the shock from my Jamaican friend's middle finger, we were picking up his energy field. His body was giving both of us a clear message as to what we needed to focus on in the reading. Once I had tuned into this energy, I could ask it what it had to say to me and receive the rest of the information intuitively.

The following page has a simple map of the energy centers on the hand. As you can see, there are areas on the hand that correspond to various issues in your life. For this week, your assignment is to practice reading these energy centers. Pay particular attention to your own hands. Your dominant hand (the one you write with) will give you information about what is

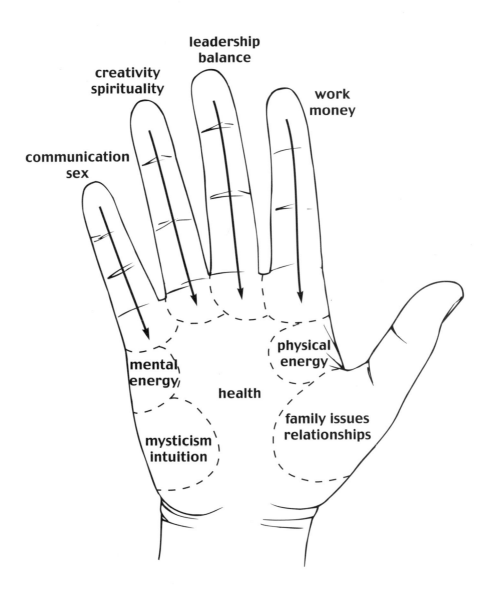

happening this very moment. Your non-dominant hand will tell you about your potential and hidden ability and desires. If you feel a tingling, cold spot, itch, or other sensation in the palms of your hand, locate the sensation, then refer to the chart to see what area of your life is asking for attention. For example, a sensation in the area around the thumb has to do with issues about the other people in your life, primarily your family. A tingling or other physical sensation under your index finger has to do with physical endurance and energy issues.

After you have located the general area of inquiry, ask your body what it wishes to tell you about that issue. For example, let's say you notice an unusual sensation under your ring finger. You look at the map of your hand and discover that this area governs creative and spiritual issues. To learn more, sit quietly for a minute and ask your intuition for more information. Listen without judgment and see what your body wishes you to know about this subject.

You can practice intuitive palmistry with your friends and family and anyone else who is open minded enough to let you feel their palm. It is often helpful for each of you to individually rub your hands together for a few seconds. This seems to wake them up in some fashion that makes the energy centers easier to feel. Then hold your hand over their palm, roughly half an inch or so above the surface. Move your hand slowly over the palm, so that you can notice any change in temperature, electrical level, or vibration. If you notice a place on your subject's palm that feels "different" (don't spend any time trying to figure out why, or you'll get out of intuition and into logic) note the location of that feeling. After locating the spot, refer to the map to determine the general area of inquiry. Finally, ask your intuition for more information about that subject.

You can also use your pendulum to read the energy and chakras of the hand. In order to do this, hold the pendulum an inch or so above the surface of the palm and slowly move it over the hand. When it starts to move back and forth or circle over a particular area, note where that area is and ask your intuition what message that part of your hand has for you. For example, I recently held a pendulum over a client's hand. It hung lifelessly most of the time, but when I held it over the area below the thumb, it began to circle widely. This area is where issues of family are located. "What is happening right now in your family that is creating a lot of emotion for you?" I asked. My client looked puzzled at first, as she was single. Then I explained that this area often held issues from childhood and she told me that she was exploring some old anger toward her mother that she had held for years. The message from the pendulum was helpful to her as it showed her in a very visible way how powerful this emotion was in her life.

You can also read the energy on your own hands, either by using your pendulum or by using one hand as the "reader" and one as the subject hand. In that case, notice the sensation that comes from the hand that is being "read." This may take some getting used to, but it is good practice for feeling energy variations and also for talking to your body.

The key to intuitive palmistry is to practice. You may need

to feel a number of palms in order to notice the subtle difference in energy centers. If you don't feel anything, ask yourself what you would feel if you could feel something. Then use that to give a mini-reading. If you are fascinated enough with palms that you want more information on the lines, shape, color, and so forth, there are many good books on the subject. But remember that the goal you are searching for is the intuitive advantage. You want to use this to aid your life, and you want to do it quickly and confidently. In order to do that, you need to let go of the rules and follow your inner knowing.

Practice reading palms this week without information other than what you have been given here. If possible, even go away from the chart and read from your soul. When you master this, you will begin to get information from everyone you shake hands with and all those you touch. You do get that information; now you need to realize it, interpret it, and use it!

12

automatic writing

On a really good day, when the writing of this book comes easily, it is almost as if an unseen hand guides my words. Other days, every phrase is an effort, the syntax seems awkward and I can't seem to remember how to spell. On those days, I wish that I could entice a handy spirit to take over and write the chapter for me. Unfortunately for me, automatic writing is another intuitive technique, not a way to get spirits to do my work for me. In essence, it is another way to gather information or knowledge from a source outside of the conscious mind. Instead of eliciting information by way of vision, emotion, or other senses, ask your higher intuitive self to give you information either by handwriting, or frequently these days by computer typing.

In case this sounds a touch too much like an occult practice to you, it is important to know that, in my opinion, you are not really consulting spirits or anything outside of yourself. While many might disagree with me, I see automatic writing as just another way to tap into the rich well of intuitive knowledge that we all carry within ourselves. This is not to say that it is not possible to "channel" entities and spirits, nor am I implying that it is wrong or "evil" to do so. I have had many experiences with channeled material and believe in the ability to contact spirits. There are many fine books, such as *Conversations With God, A Course In Miracles,* and the Seth materials, that are considered to be channeled and which are extremely useful and wise. However, it is not necessary to contact anyone or thing outside of yourself in order to obtain the best information. Automatic writing, like all intuitive techniques, should be done in a way that is comfortable to you and that fits into your belief system.

This week, you will explore your unconscious by way of writing. It is prepared for in the same fashion we have used for several weeks. You will go to your sacred and silent space, where you will put yourself in a focus state. Then, you will invite your higher self or intuition or whatever you feel comfortable calling it, to speak to you by allowing your hand to move freely over a piece of paper.

Have a large amount of unlined blank paper in front of you. Become as relaxed and focused as you can and then ask yourself, "What do I want to know?" You can use one of the questions you have prepared earlier, or you can say, "Give me direction on..." In any event, write your question or area of inquiry on the top of your first piece of paper. Hold your pen or pencil lightly in your hand, close your eyes, and put yourself in a slight trance or focus state. And wait.

If no thoughts come to you, slowly begin to move your hand in a circular motion, mimicking the act of writing. If thoughts appear in your mind, write them down. Do not monitor the movement of these thoughts. Do not be concerned about "making something up." Simply keep writing. All of the data that will come to you comes to you from your intuition and imagination. Do not worry about which area the information is coming from; simply let it flow.

Don't force this process. You may find that you will write for ten or fifteen minutes, or perhaps only for a minute or so. Either way is fine. When you are finished, the information will cease to flow. Then, of course, you will stop. After you are finished, read the message. You may be very surprised to discover what you have written.

When I teach this exercise in my classes, someone almost always feels that they have received a message from a spirit or deceased loved one. Often the information is very specific or has defining characteristics that feel as if it was from someone else. Honor this if happens to you but do not elicit it or expect it. Allow the flow to give you what you need, not what you want. Your intuition has the ability to get information from many sources. If you spend a great deal of time pondering where or how you know something, you can get so lost in the process that you lose the advantage. Take what you get as a gift from your higher self, which can communicate on levels we don't fully understand. Don't allow either fear or desire to taint the exercise.

Another way to do automatic writing is to sit quietly in front of your computer in a blank document mode of word processing. Write your question or area of inquiry at the top of the page, and then rest your hands lightly on the keys. Slowly, you will find yourself typing, often at a more rapid pace than you are capable of in a fully conscious state. Let your fingers go as they will. It often helps to keep your eyes closed and to be totally unconcerned about whether you are hitting the right keys or not.

Suddenly, your hands will quit. At that time, the fun begins. I do this often, especially when I have a thorny issue about which I wish some guidance. I am often surprised at what messages I receive. Often there were parts that, because my hands got off the correct placement, made no sense to me at all. Other times, there will be pieces that are beautiful, almost poetic in their meaning. Sometimes I feel that I am forcing it, typing only what I wish to hear. If I let this self-judgment go, and keep typing, I get to a point where my brain quiets and my hands continue to move.

Keep what you have written or typed, whether you feel it has meaning or not. Often consulting these writings months later will give you insights you would not have gotten immediately after the event. As with all intuitive practices, automatic writing will work for some and not for others. Use this week to practice. If writing by hand is uncomfortable, use a keyboard.

If both typing and handwriting feel difficult, you can even try dictating into a tape recorder. At this stage of your intuitive training, you may be too self-conscious to do that, but if it works for you, automatic dictation can be great fun as well.

The key to this week's lesson is to try a technique that is new and different. As with all of the practices, continue to use it if it is helpful and remove it from your life if it is not. But, first give it a good try. You won't be able to fully get the "feel" of the experience until you have tried it two or three times. If, after that number of times, it still feels foreign or useless, go on to another technique, knowing that you have given it a good effort and that you can return to using it at another time if it seems appropriate.

13

seeing auras

"Do you see auras?" This is a question asked of me frequently as I teach intuitive practices. My answer is always the same. "Yes," I say, "and so do you." It is my belief that everyone can see auras. I also believe that, as children, we see and acknowledge them clearly. Look at a crayon picture drawn by a young child. Often, around their stick figures, they will color in a halo or aura. It is common for children under the age of five or six to paint colors around the bodies they draw. If you have contact with young children, ask them if they see colors around people, or give them some crayons and ask them to draw in the colors that they see around you. It is great fun to see your son color you with pink around your head or green emanating through your arms. Unfortunately as children age, their parents, teachers, and friends gradually convince them that what they are seeing is not really there. Finally, the children too no longer believe that they see what they see.

I have been training people to see auras for many years. After only a few minutes of explanation, only a handful of my students cannot see auras. Why? Because I am not really teaching them to see something new, I am merely reminding them of what they have always seen. Most people don't know that they see auras because they have a faulty idea of what an aura is. My definition of an aura is the electrical and magnetic field that surrounds every living being. This field is measurable and observable through many sophisticated machines such as a MRI, but is also easily seen with the human eye. Sometimes called your Chi or Prana or halo, your human energy field or aura is distinctive to you and easily observable to both you and others.

This week, your assignment is to learn to see auras, to practice observing them, and to ask your intuition what meaning each aura has to you. The easiest way to learn to see an aura is to get one or two volunteers, preferably wearing a white or light-colored shirt, to stand in front of a white wall in a well lit room without shadows. Have your volunteer sway very slowly back and forth while you focus, not directly at, but slightly past, the person. It helps to use soft, slightly unfocused eyes and to look a little behind the person.

You will notice a slight halo or aura, usually white or light colored, that extends two to six inches around the person. This halo, often called the envelope, is, in fact, the person's aura. It is not a shadow but an envelope of energy that moves with the person as he or she moves. In fact, it looks a little like the heat energy that you can observe on the surface of a car on a warm day. If you continue to watch this aura, you may see colors coming and going. For instance, I often see slight yellow hues around a person's head or green around the shoulders.

Often, people are simply expecting too much. They say to me, "Well, I have always seen that. I thought an aura would be much brighter and more impressive." Don't be disappointed; the color of auras is seldom as bright as is portrayed in books or pictures. Most people's auras do generally contain colors, however, and these colors fluctuate minute by minute. As you become more practiced and watch for auras, you will see the colors more clearly. By watching these colors, and also by watching the size of the aura, you can tell a great deal about what is going on with the person.

Don't worry too much about what the colors mean or the interpretation of the colors. There are many good books available on aura colors, particularly as they related to the chakras of the body. In general, yellow tends to show thinking or intellect, green is often about healing, pink or red is emotional, and violet is spiritual. A gray or dark aura can sometimes indicate illness or sadness. Your intuition will give you all the information you need to interpret these colors. If you see a tinge of pink around a person, remember it is probably about an emotion, and then ask yourself, "What does this say?" Perhaps you will discover that you sense anger, or maybe you will feel love instead. Trust your intuition to be correct on this, and ask it for more information if it seems appropriate. The key is to see the auras, and then to ask yourself, "What is this person's aura telling me?" You will get a much better reading by this method than simply memorizing what each color means and sticking with someone else's definition.

When you look at a person's aura, you are reading them at a soul level. This cannot help but have an effect on you at a soul level as well. A few years ago, I was one of the keynote speakers at an international metaphysical and spiritual conference. Although I speak worldwide, and conduct intuition training for many diverse groups, it is rare for me to feel so at home at a conference as I felt at this symposium. My talk had been accepted with love and I felt surrounded by like-minded individuals. The entire week had been more of a vacation than a job for me and I was sorry to see it come to an end.

I had been told about the healing service that was considered by many to be the highlight of the week. It was held on the last night of the symposium. I had been invited to join the forty or so healers who took their place on the stage, but I had respectfully declined. I was a speaker, teacher and palmist, but I did not consider myself a healer. Besides, I wished to experience this from an observer's point of view and, perhaps experience some healing for myself.

I sat in one of the front rows, transfixed by the spectacle unfolding in front of me. The healers came from dozens of countries and incorporated as many healing traditions. Shamanistic healing was done next to those healing from a Christian tradition. Some healers prayed, some used touch, others moved in a dance fashion. Beauty, power, and love hung in the air. Earlier, I had decided to ask the universe for improvement of my eyesight. As I aged my near vision was becoming more and more foggy and, while it was correctable with lenses, it was causing me eyestrain and difficulty. I was one of the first of nearly four hundred to go onto the stage to experience the healing. I was directed to the chair in front of a minister with whom I had become acquainted earlier in the week. I knew that we both came from the Christian tradition and felt comfortable opening myself to her ministrations.

I could sense her hands stroking my aura, even though there was no actual touch. I silently prayed for clear sight as the power in her hands magnified. I felt a warm white light enter me through my crown, engulfing my body down to my toes. I could only sense that the Holy Spirit had touched me—then it was gone. I stood shakily and headed across the stage to my seat. As I stood momentarily at the stairs leading down off the stage, I gazed out at the audience. I was transfixed by the sight. All of the hundreds of people in the auditorium were glowing with a white light and were connected by thin golden strands. The sight was so beautiful that I was moved to tears.

As the service continued the audience filed past me on their way to the stage. As each person walked past me, I stared in awe. Never had I seen such beauty or felt such love. At that moment I was connected to everyone in the room. I knew everything about each person, all their fears, challenges, and dreams—and all I saw was beauty. Even after the service, the glow continued. There was a reception at which we chatted and drank coffee. At one point a woman approached me to ask for clarification about a palm reading I had given her earlier. As I again looked at her hand, the sensation of knowingness continued. Her life was opened to me in a way I had never before experienced—and it was exquisite!

The next day, the glow was gone and my intuitive knowing was back to its normal level. But I had been changed in a way that I still cannot fully explain. My near vision had not been healed, rather I had been given a new vision. My prayer for clear sight had been granted in a way that I still cannot fully comprehend.

This week, practice seeing auras wherever you go. Open yourself up to the magnificence of the energy fields that surround every living thing—people, plants, and animals. Ask for clear vision and trust that your higher self will show you the truth in all you see.

14

intuitive dowsing

Some of my favorite intuitive toys are dowsing rods. I think I like them so much because people turn into little children when handed a set of rods. They laugh, play, and generally have a great time. This light-heartedness is a wonderful place to discover intuitive ability for it takes people out of their grown-up skeptical persona. I always carry dowsing rods with me when I train police officers. I love to watch while a group uniformed officers point dowsing rods at each other and roar with laughter. Still, there is a serious and useful part to the use of these rods. So this week, be prepared to have some fun. You are going to dowse everyone and everything you know.

Dowsing rods are very simple to make and use. If you enjoy using them, you will probably want to purchase a professional set. You can order them from the American Society of Dowsers, or find them at some new age bookstores. But for this week, you can make your own set from a pair of wire coat hangers. Take the hangers and straighten them out, then use a wire cutter or clippers to cut the wires until they are twelve to eighteen inches long. Bend one end of the hanger into an L-shape, with the small L-section being just long enough to hold comfortably. The two rods should be approximately the same lengths. When you are finished you should have two rods which you can hold by the L-handles and have about a foot or so of wire pointing out. You can then create a holder for the handles out of an index card or any other substance that will allow the handle to swing freely. The easiest thing to do is to take an index card and tape it into a small circle that will just fit around the handle. The goal is to have a set of rods that swing freely while you hold them as if you were pointing a set of pistols.

Once you have your dowsing rods made, you need to master using them. Hold them by the handles so they swing effortlessly. Hold them away from your body enough so that they don't pick up your energy field and swing back to you. You will need to practice with them for awhile until you can get them to stay still while holding them out parallel with each other and at a 90-degree angle from your body. Once you have the hang of that, you are ready to dowse!

Dowsing has been around for centuries. The most common use of dowsing, and the one that most people have heard of, is that of dowsing for water. Water dowsers use rods or even tree twigs to read the energy of water and locate a spot to dig a well. Despite scientific skepticism, dowsing is used in many areas as the most efficient way to find underground water.

Dowsing rods are used for other purposes as well. My husband's cousin, as down-to-earth and skeptical a man as they come, works for a small town, plowing snow, and doing other types of municipal work. I was amused to discover that one of his jobs was to dowse the local cemetery for remains before a grave was dug. It turns out dowsing for human remains is the best way of determining that there are no unmarked graves to be disturbed.

This week, though, you aren't going to dowse for water or bones (unless of course you wish to). You will be dowsing for human energy fields. As you learned last week, every living thing has an energy field which can be seen and felt once you know what you are looking for. Using dowsing rods to find and measure this field is fascinating, as it gives visible proof that energy fields exist. Even my most skeptical students are amazed at the results.

You will need to enlist some volunteers for this week's lesson. This isn't as difficult as it might seem, however. Most people find this enjoyable, even if they don't believe in the premise. Children are wonderful subjects and they have a natural ability to control their energy field that is great to watch. Find one or two friends or family members and ask them to stand fifteen feet away from you. Hold your dowsing rods out in front of you, far enough away from your body that they aren't swinging back to pick up your own field. Then walk slowly toward your subject. When you reach that person's energy field or aura, the rods will naturally swing out or together. How they swing is individual to the person and will vary from person to person and dowser to dowser.

Just seeing this phenomena is enough to make most people believe in the human energy field. But, the really useful part is discovering that, even though you may not even have known you had an energy field, you have complete control of it. To demonstrate this, ask your subject to consciously send out their energy field. They may ask you how to do this. Just respond that they know how to do it. Like everything in life, it is done with intent—you just do it. Once they have sent out their energy field, walk slowly toward them once again. In all likelihood, the rods will move when you are much farther away from the person then the first time you measured their field. They have, without knowing how, expanded their aura.

Now, have them experiment with pulling their energy field in. We unconsciously hold our energy field in whenever we feel angry, sad, or threatened. Ask your subject to think of someone or something they are angry with, then repeat the exercise. When I do this demonstration, I often have to walk right up to the person, even touching them with the rods, before I hit their energy field. Please remember never to leave the person in that angry spot. Ask them to forgive or love the very thing they were angry about and show them how their aura expands. This is a very visible demonstration of the power of our emotions on our bodies.

You can practice with your rods in various ways. I sometimes have people hold a crystal or eat a small amount of sugar to demonstrate the effect certain substances have on the energy field. But the most important use of this practice is to show you how much control you have over a field of which you weren't even aware.

When I train police, I always tell them to send their energy field out in threatening situations. Of course, officers can't bring dowsing rods with them on their beats, (although wouldn't it be fascinating if they did), but they can be aware of the impact their energy field has on others. By sending out their fields, rather than the natural reaction of pulling it in, they are much less likely to encourage confrontation. People just intuitively step out of others' auras unless invited. Remember that the intuitive part of you can read these fields without the use of the dowsing rods. The rods are only a learning device, to show you that the human energy field exists and that you are in control of it.

Learning to control your energy field is like having a secret weapon against boundary intruders, tailgaters, and psychic vampires. When you consciously send out your aura, you are creating a bubble of protection around yourself. An interesting experiment is to send your energy field out when you are on a crowded elevator and watch the people around you move out of your field. I also create a field around my car whenever I am being tailgated and watch the other car back away from me.

Whenever you feel threatened or frightened, try sending out your aura. It is a useful tool when walking in an unfamiliar part of town, or even just going to a job interview. I always extend my aura as wide as possible when I am giving a lecture to a large group. In that setting, I want to appear in control and powerful, and the audience will see and intuit the size of my energy field. Plus, I gain a sense of confidence and control which helps me speak with authority.

This week, enjoy using your dowsing rods in many situations. If you truly enjoy them, you will probably wish to purchase a professional pair, since coat hangers are ugly, though effective. Also, practice the control of your own energy field. Send it out to those you love, but also project it out when you want space. Those you love or wish to attract will be happy to join their energy fields with yours. Those you wish to keep at bay will stand back and give you the space you desire. It is a wonderfully effective way to create boundaries in a loving and private fashion.

15

feeling the human energy field

Of all the groups I have trained, the one which presented me with the most unique challenge was that of a group of corrections workers, nurses, and doctors at a facility for the mentally ill and dangerous. After all, they worked all day with people who hear and see things that no one else does. How did I convince them that mentally healthy "normal" people also could see and hear things, but on an intuitive level that could be used to their advantage? I started by discussing the human energy field. "The human energy field," I explained, "surrounds every human being. It is caused by our electrical and magnetic energy and is measurable by many medical scientific instruments." So far, so good. This was a group used to dealing with x-rays and MRI's and other testing devices that measure things about the body which aren't visible with our ordinary senses.

"What you may not be aware of," I continued, "is that you are able to sense and see this energy field without the use of mechanical tools." As I walked among the participants, I decided to do a brief demonstration. "For example, each person's energy field can by felt by holding the palms of your hands two or three inches away from their body." I explained that it was helpful to "wake up" your nerve endings by rubbing your hands together for a minute or so. Then, at random, I approached a woman in the audience and after asking her permission to do so, I slowly held my hands, palm side down, over her head. I continued to move my hands down the side of her head and shoulders, while discussing how each person's energy field has a unique feel. "After you have accustomed yourself to the person's energy," I explained, "you can sense certain areas that may feel different than others. For example, there may be a spot on the person's body that is warmer or colder, or seems to vibrate at a faster or slower level." Then I paused as my hands rested an inch above her shoulders. Without knowing I was doing so, I asked, "What is wrong with your left shoulder?"

The woman turned around and looked at me with a mixture of wonderment and doubt. "Why do you ask that?" she said. I told her I wasn't sure, and again brought my hands over her head, down her neck and around her shoulders. "Your left shoulder is colder and has a much slower vibration than does your right," I said. She then told the class that she had been suffering from severe pain in that shoulder for years, and had just had surgery to correct the problem. "I don't know how you could have known that," she stated, as if to suggest I had checked medical records before doing the training.

I was a little shaken by the experience as well. I do not bill myself as a medical intuitive, and have no medical training or knowledge. I believe that intuition can tell us many things, but, as practicing lawyer, I never attempt a medical diagnosis. My legal malpractice carrier is much happier when I stick to giving legal advice. Still, it was a good illustration of the human energy field, and certainly did get the groups' attention.

Soon after I had done this demonstration, we broke into pairs and the participants practiced on each other. The reports that came back were definitely positive. Even if they weren't certain what they were feeling, almost everyone in the group left the exercise realizing that they were feeling something. In just a few minutes, they had learned to feel the energy field that surrounds not just humans, but every living thing.

Throughout the ages, this energy field has been seen and felt by those of us aware enough to look for it. Also called the aura, prana, or Chi, it is not as esoteric as it is sometimes portrayed to be. Put down this book for a minute and vigorously rub your hands together for a minute or so. Then spread them about eighteen inches apart. Slowly bring them back together, palm sides facing each other, until you reach a point where you feel a slightly resistance or spongy feel. It may take you a few times of practicing until you can feel this spot, but once you do, you will know it from then on. You have just felt your own aura or energy field.

Now that you know what it feels like, your job this week is to feel the energy fields of other living things. Practice on your open-minded family and friends. To begin with, don't try to interpret what you feel, just practice until you are certain that you are familiar with the feeling of the energy. Notice that different people's field have a different feeling. Notice also that the energy field changes at different points on the body.

You can practice on your pets as well. Animals love to have their auras stroked; and this activity has the added benefit of not having your sanity questioned. Once you are confident that you are, in fact, feeling energy, you can add intuition into the exercise. This time, while stroking someone's field, ask yourself what the field has to say to you. If you get a picture in your mind's eye or a thought, be brave enough to check that impression out with the other person. You may be wrong, but you will never know until you are courageous enough to ask.

Sometimes, you may feel the other person's emotions or even their physical pain or symptoms. If this happens, make sure that whether you chose to share that with the other person or not, you do not take on these feelings or sensations. Be aware of what is you and what is not you, and keep only your own emotions and feelings as part of you. (For more information on how to do this, read the chapter on psychic protection later in this book.)

Jeanie came to one of my intuition classes even though she had taken a severe fall the night before. She had hit her forehead and been to the emergency room where she had received numerous stitches. Her face was bruised and swollen and she had a terrible headache. "I don't know how long I can stay," she said. "But I just didn't want to miss this class." I don't teach healing, nor do I consider myself to be a healer, but the class made the decision that we should do what we could to help Jeanie make it through the day.

One by one, we held our hands over her injury. It was a very good lesson in energy fields, as the spot on her head had a heavy pulsing sensation and coolness that everyone in the class could feel. We decided to intentionally warm up the spot and send calmness to the pulsing. After we did so, Jeanie reported a noticeable easing of the pain. She was able it make it through the rest of the day. I saw her a few weeks later and she told me that her doctor had been amazed at the speed in which healing had taken place. Jeanie had become a believer in the power of the mind for healing.

There are a lot of unanswered questions about that story. Did we "heal" Jeanie or was her belief in the process strong enough that she healed herself? Did anything happen at all, or was it all just a natural healing which coincidentally happened at the same time? To my mind, the answers to those questions don't matter and so I will leave the proof of hands-on healing to the scientists and researchers to decide. I take a very pragmatic approach to intuition, healing, and all matters unproved. If it works and gives me a better life, I use it. If it doesn't, I don't.

There is little scientific argument, these days, with the premise that the mind has an enormous effect on the physical body. You can demonstrate this to yourself—plus impress your skeptical friends—by mastering the ancient Qigong practice of growing your fingers. I first saw this demonstrated by a Chinese Qigong master who implied that it was a very difficult feat that could only be done after years of study. A few years later I learned to do it quickly by myself, and discovered that it is less about mysticism and more about the power of our minds to affect our bodies.

Hold your hands together, palms touching with the lines of the wrists matching up. Notice if any of the fingers of either hand are longer on one hand or the other. Once you have observed the length of your fingers on one hand in comparison to the other, chose one of the hands to use to grow your fingers. It doesn't matter which hand you chose, just remember which one it is. Take the hand you have chosen to use and hold it front of you in a comfortable fashion. Place yourself in a focus state and concentrate on the fingers of that hand. Slowly breathe in and out. On each out breath say to yourself, "my fingers are growing longer." Concentrate on lengthening your fingers, feel the energy course through the fingers, and intend that the fingers on that hand grow longer and longer. Continue to breathe and repeat the phrase for at least two or three minutes.

When you are finished, you will know it intuitively. Then, place your hands together again and notice whether the fingers on the hand on which you concentrated are now longer than they were when you first compared hands. Most people are able to grow their fingers enough to get a visible difference. If you didn't, don't be discouraged. Just keep trying until you are able to do so. Like all the exercises in this book, it might take a little time to get the technique down.

Don't worry about walking around forever with fingers of unequal length. The growth of the fingers is a temporary thing and they will go back to their usual length in just a few minutes. What you did was not magic; it was a concrete example of the power of your mind over your physical body. As you concentrated on your fingers, blood and other fluids went to the tips of your fingers, temporarily filling them and causing them to lengthen. As soon as your attention turned elsewhere, the blood and fluids returned to normal and the fingers did the same.

To me, that is the very essence of the intuitive advantage. Learning to control your mind and body intuitively can positively affect your life in many ways, even your physical health. In the case of Jeanie's "healing," whatever we did for her eased her pain and allowed her to do what she wanted to do. When you learn to read and control the energy fields of your body, you too can learn to ease pain and feel more in control. Reading the fields of others will give you information as to how to deal with them, and perhaps help them as well.

16

remote viewing

While sitting quietly on my living room sofa, I begin each day with a time of meditation, prayer, and study. I generally start by reading a few meditations or sentences from a spiritual text, then I stare into a candle to quiet my mind, and spend ten or fifteen minutes in a type of trance, stilling as much as possible the chatter of my mind. Gradually, my mind will begin to focus on various topics or persons again, and I have learned not to stop this process. Instead, I use the next few minutes to practice intuition. If I think of a particular person, for example, I will ask my mind to show me that person. Often, I will see a picture of that person in my mind's eye. I will note where the person is, what she is doing, and what her energy pattern looks like. Sometimes we will even engage in a conversation.

Later that day, I often find myself talking to this person, and if I know them well enough to feel comfortable doing so, I will tell them of my meditation and what I saw. It is surprising how frequently my "visions" are accurate and how helpful they tend to be to both me and the person I was viewing.

I had done this exercise in some form or another for many years before I learned that it had a name. I was lecturing on a cruise ship and one of the other presenters was speaking on remote viewing. I had heard about remote viewing before, of course, but had never considered doing it. I thought of it as a psychic spy sort of thing which didn't appeal to me at all. So, when I went to the lecture, I was surprised to learn that I had been remotely viewing my friends and family for years!

Remote viewing has received a lot of attention lately after it was revealed that the CIA and Defense Department of the United States Government used and trained remote viewers for over twenty years to do espionage. It was also learned that the Soviet Union had used so-called psychic spying success- fully since before World War II. These revelations spurred a slew of books and articles and prompted several agencies to create training institutes. Many of these training programs imply that remote viewing takes years to master and can be done only by highly trained psychics. Because of this, most people, even those who consider themselves to be intuitive, believe that remote viewing is too difficult or complicated to be of use. This, in my opinion, is a false assumption that keeps us from getting valuable information.

Remote viewing at its simplest is seeing something in your

mind's eye which you cannot see with your physical eyes. This definition removes some of the mystique surrounding remote viewing and brings it to a level that many of us practice. You have, perhaps, thought of your child at school, picturing her as she went about her day. How did you do this? Was it only your imagination or were you, in fact, viewing her as she truly was? You have the ability to remotely view many things, people, and objects. However, in order for this to be useful to you, you need to keep in mind some simple instructions.

Preparation for remote viewing is the same as it is with all intuitive practices. First and foremost, you must believe that it is possible and that you can do it. Second, you should place yourself in your focus state, relaxing your tongue or using whatever other technique works best for you. And, of course, you will need to practice remote viewing as often as possible.

If you are a person who loses or misplaces things, you have a perfect avenue for remote viewing practice. The next time you can't find your keys, for example, sit quietly rather than rushing around in a searching frenzy. Hold a pen or pencil lightly in hand with a blank sheet of paper in front of you. Tell yourself that you are going to view the location of the lost item and then wait patiently for a picture to appear in your mind's eye. You will get some sort of message. It is easiest, of course, if you get your intuitive messages as pictures, but you can practice remote viewing even if you are primarily a feeling-based or word-based intuitive. In those cases, you will write down the feelings you receive or the words that come to your mind. On your paper, draw the picture you see, write the word you hear or describe the feeling you get—but do not analyze these images or thoughts.

The key to remote viewing is detachment. Your unconscious intuitive mind will provide you with an image or idea which may not "make sense" to your conscious mind. The conscious mind will then immediately jump in and attempt to translate or explain the image. For example, you may see a round ball of light. Your conscious mind will wish to define this image, perhaps as a light bulb, the sun, or a yellow ball. The minute you begin naming your image, your conscious mind begins to fill in the blanks, often in a completely false direction. Then, in typical fashion, it tells you that this whole thing is stupid and couldn't possibly work anyhow.

At this stage of your remote viewing exercise it is crucial not to interpret, define, or identify your perceptions. You should just draw or write out the impressions as you see them. Don't think about how it works or if it works—just do it. Keep going until you have a strong impression that you are finished. Then sit quietly for a few more minutes in order to verify that you are, in fact, through with the exercise.

Now it is time to enlist your conscious mind, impatiently waiting in the background. Look at what you have written or drawn and ask yourself, "What does this mean to me?" Our unconscious speaks to us symbolically and each of us uses different symbols for different items. Red, for example, may mean anger to one person, passion to another, and freedom to a third. Since this is your mind, you must interpret what these symbols mean for yourself.

In the case of the missing keys, you may have drawn a place which looks vaguely familiar and to which you can go to look for them. Perhaps you have a series of words, which you need to interpret, keeping in mind your goal of finding your keys. Finally, remember the intuitive element of action and use your information to help you go to the place you envision—and search!

You will more than likely find that you need to practice this exercise often before it becomes a useful tool. Don't be discouraged by this. The first time you hit a golf ball you probably didn't have a great drive. Don't expect your intuition to be immediately proficient at a brand new task.

Nonetheless, I have been repeatedly overwhelmed by the success my students have with remote viewing. In preparation for these exercises, I generally cut a photograph from a magazine, mount it on a piece of cardboard, and place it in a manila envelope. Then, during the remote viewing class, I take the envelope out of my briefcase, hold it in front of the class and ask them to focus on the envelope and draw whatever picture, image, or thought comes to mind. I have done this exercise dozens of times with many diverse groups. In every group, one or more of my students draws almost the exact picture depicted in the photograph!

A few months ago I was teaching a class in intuition at a workshop sponsored by a chamber of commerce. The attendees were all successful business people, mostly rather skeptical, but with a desire to improve their intuitive skills. When I explained the remote viewing exercise, there was open doubt on their faces. I heard mumbles of "that's impossible," and "I can't do that." Still, they all participated in the exercise.

After giving instructions, I pulled out the envelope from the briefcase resting on the table behind me. I held up the envelope with the instructions "focus on the envelope," then laid it back on the table. For ten minutes or so, the class attempted to view the picture contained in the envelope. Periodically, I would remind them to focus on the envelope.

While many remote viewers spend hours focusing while in training, I have found that beginners are exhausted after just a few minutes. After that time, their conscious mind barges back in, interpreting and analyzing. So, in my beginning classes we keep this exercise fairly brief.

After ten minutes, I asked the class to tell me what they saw. As they called out their descriptions, I wrote or drew them on a whiteboard behind me. Shortly into this exercise, I noticed a peculiar pattern developing. There seemed to be two very different scenes being described.

After we were finished we opened the envelope. About half of the class had successfully described at least some of the elements in the photograph, but the other half of the class had missed completely. While this was not terribly unusual, what was unusual was that the so-called "wrong" descriptions were all strikingly similar. I was stumped.

Suddenly I remembered that, in preparing for this class, I had made two separate manila envelopes, in case we had extra time and needed an additional exercise. I removed the unused envelope from my briefcase, pulled out the photograph, and was stunned to see that half of the class had successfully seen and described the picture which had been unused, lying in another envelope in my briefcase!

This was a very good lesson for me on teaching and intuition. When I instructed the class to "focus on the envelope," I was not specific as to which envelope. Of course, the envelope in my briefcase was just as accessible to intuitive knowing as the envelope lying on the table. I had been given a powerful teaching on the importance of specificity in intuitive practices. If you don't ask for the exact thing you wish to know, you won't get what you want. It is very similar to the old computer-programming adage of "garbage in—garbage out." In this case, it is important to remember "garbage asked for—garbage received."

My most memorable experience with remote viewing came while writing this book. I received a telephone call from my literary agent early on a Monday morning. A sister of a friend of hers, she told me, was missing. The missing woman and her niece had left Minneapolis on the previous Friday afternoon with plans to meet the woman's husband at a campground in northern Minnesota that evening. When they didn't show up at the arranged time, he had called the police and filed a missing persons' report. Three days later, the pair still had not been heard from and their family was frantic. In desperation, they called my agent asking if she knew any psychics.

"I don't do that sort of thing," I told her. "And even if I did, nothing is ever 100% certain." My agent assured me that the family understood that, but were so desperate that they were willing to try anything—even me. Finally, I agreed to look for the missing pair. I put myself into a focus state and immediately was given a vision of two people, a middle-aged woman with dark hair and a young blonde girl. I was also shown an older model blue-gray automobile. "Is that them?" I asked. My agent didn't know the missing people personally, but she agreed to call the family to ask.

A few minutes later my telephone rang again. "Yes," she said. "The sister of my friend has dark hair and the girl is blonde—and their car is bluish-gray!" With that verification, I felt I had to continue to search for them. I immediately saw both women in my mind's eye, and was both relieved and surprised to see that they appeared fine. "The woman seems confused and somewhat angry," I told my agent, "but the girl is happy. I don't see any sign of abduction or injury. I don't know why they haven't called, but they look to be fine."

After I hung up the telephone, I sat for awhile. My lawyer-like conscious mind then decided to berate me. "How could you know that?" it said. "All the facts lean toward injury or criminal behavior. There is no history of mental illness or alcohol abuse or any reason for them to disappear for three days without a trace. Why did you give the family false hope? What if they don't search as hard because of what you said?" I spent most of the rest of the day psychologically beating myself up for not using a logical analysis of the situation. At 9:00 PM the telephone rang once more. My agent's voice said simply, "I'm not sure what happened, but they just walked in the door, safe and surprised that anyone was worried about them."

This incident was very meaningful to me. Of course, it illustrated the validity of remote viewing, but, after years of experience, I was actually confident about that. What it showed me was that, at a core level, I still didn't fully trust intuition as being as valuable as logic. I made a vow then and there to trust myself in all ways and to speak my intuitive truth even when it went against prevailing wisdom. I urge you to do the same.

This week, spend a few minutes every day doing remote viewing. You can do this in many ways. Try finding lost items. Locate your child or spouse at school or work and see what they are doing. Enlist a friend to help you and use the picture in the manila envelope exercise. Sit quietly before going to a new restaurant or friend's house and ask yourself what the building looks like, what color the furniture is, and what feeling you get from the location.

If at all possible, try to get feedback. Call your friend, tell her your impressions, and ask if you are correct. Go to the building you were viewing and look for elements that match what you saw, practice with the manila envelope until you can keep your mind from interpreting. Enjoy this exercise, play with it, and remember that, as with all things in life, you will get more proficient the more you do it.

17

preparing a quest box

This week, you will create an intuitive tool which I call a Quest(ion) Box. To do this, you should find a container large enough to accommodate slips of paper and into which you can insert your hand comfortably. It can be a shoebox, a cookie tin, or a pre-made purchased box or container. While not necessary, it is fun to decorate this box with images and symbols of your intuitive quest. Some of my students spend a lot of time preparing their box, searching for the just the right photos, articles, small stones, feathers, or shells to glue on top of the box, or even on the inside of the cover. If you wish, you can also put small meaningful items that symbolize your quest inside the box.

The purpose of this decorating is merely to remind you that each time you use or look at your quest box, you are on a sacred pursuit of intuitive truth. This truth is sacred, as is the quest itself. The box itself does not create magic, although it may seem to sometimes. Your intuitive mind is the magician, pulling answers out of a hat for your advantage. Like all sacred things, your quest and your box should be treated with respect.

Now you will fill your box with your questions. Write each question on a separate piece of white paper and fold them in a way which does not let you see the content of the question when you draw the paper from the box. As in all intuitive exercises, the preparation of the questions is the most important task. I have some difficulties with this part of the work. I am a very impulsive and impatient person and I like to move quickly and get on with things. It is particularly important for me, therefore, to sit quietly and meditatively and to work on my questions with reverence and thought.

You may place as many questions into the box as you wish, the more the better. You will find that this exercise works best when you lose self-centeredness and ask for guidance for others, for society, and for the world. However, this is your box, private and sacred. Into this box can go your deepest fears, your strongest longings. No one will see these questions but you. Make sure that you keep your quest box in a place that is "off limits" to others, and make sure that your housemates are aware of this. You need to be confident that you can place any question in this box in safety and confidentiality.

Let these questions sit for a few days, if you can wait that long. This waiting functions like yeast does for bread. The questions seem almost to change, to leaven and transform into something else. When you are ready, return to your quest box. To do this exercise you must be alone, in a quiet undisturbed place for at least a half-hour or more. Turn off the phone, hang a do-not-disturb sign on your door and do whatever you need to feel comfortable and serene. If it helps, you can experiment with soft music, candles, incense, or other mood setting devices. These items are not required for the exercise to work, but they do give a sense of reverence and importance to your task. I have found that silence works best for me. I am distracted by music and incense makes me sneeze. It is up to you to find your own favorite setting and create your own sacred space.

If you have waited a few days since placing your questions in the box, your logical brain will probably have forgotten some of the content although your intuitive mind forgets nothing. Place a sheet of blank paper or your intuition notebook in front of you and hold a pen or pencil lightly in your hand. Before drawing a slip from the box, enter into as meditative a state as possible. Practice the tongue loosening exercise we discussed earlier or use whatever other technique works for you. Clear your mind of all expectations, hopes, fears, and memories. Tell yourself that the answers do not matter, it is the quest that is important. Then draw out a slip.

Holding the slip in your hand, note how you feel. Put a word or words to your feelings, no matter how difficult this is for you. Are you impatient, angry, hot, happy? Write these feelings down on your paper in as much detail as you can. Then ask your mind for a message. Sit quietly until a thought comes or until you see a picture in your mind's eye. Try not to consider which question you may be answering, just immerse yourself in the joy of the experience. If the thought is unclear or the picture foggy, ask for more detail. For example, if you see a road, ask your mind where the road is or what direction it runs. Then ask your mind to take you down that road, noting what happens.

You can follow this line of questioning as long as it feels right. Some people create an entire story full of intricate characters, color, and pageantry. Others get only vague words or feelings. Both are good and neither is preferable to the other. How your intuition speaks to you is your personal and unique gift, just like the color of your hair or eyes. It is highly individual.

Eventually your intuition will give you some sort of sign or message that you are finished. Don't push to get more than that. While the contents of your vision or thought are fresh in your mind, write them down on your paper, giving as much detail as possible. Small things here can be very important so don't omit anything, even if it seems unimportant.

After you have written as much as you can remember, sit quietly for a few moments, reviewing the experience. Most people recall a few more items, others just relish the relaxing feeling. Finally, open the folded slip of paper and read the question. Ask your intuition for guidance in interpreting your reading. Take time to ponder the implications and, if you wish, write out your interpretation. Then give yourself time to let the experience sink in, ending the session by thanking your intuition for the gift it has given to you.

Sometimes the meaning of your reading is immediately evident, other times it may take weeks or months for the interpretation to become clear. I used this exercise a few years ago, drawing the question: "What direction should I go in my life's work?" After writing my intuitive messages down, I read this question and chuckled to see that I had written the words "rising sun" and "east" among other words. I laughed to think that my intuition had taken my request so literally that it told me to go in an actual compass direction. Other than the giggle value, I didn't feel that I got much help from that reading.

Several months later, I was invited to join a group trip to China. I agreed somewhat impulsively and ended up having an adventure that was life-changing. It was only after I returned that I remembered my reading and its advice to "go east." My intuition had given me as good advice as it could based on my poorly-worded question. While the interpretation of that advice wasn't completely clear for several months, the memory of that message may very well have been a factor in my sudden decision to join the group. Never underestimate the power of your intuitive mind to give you good guidance, even when you don't completely understand it at the time!

The most important work you will do this week is creating your box and your questions. The actual creation of the box can give you intuitive messages as well. When I made mine many years ago, I found myself covering the box with pictures of the ocean and beaches and placing a seashell inside. Since I live in Minnesota, a long way away from the ocean, I wasn't sure as to why that symbolism called me. Since that time, though, the ocean has played a huge role in my life. I work for several cruise lines and resorts, lecturing on intuition. Despite spending a lot of time working in the Caribbean and South and Central America, I still find myself drawn there for vacations or whenever I need rest and relaxation. My intuition knew about this long before my conscious mind was aware of it. After I learned this about myself, I made a conscious decision to surround myself with symbols of the ocean's healing. It was only then that I remembered that, as a small girl, I collected seashells. Sometimes our childhood hobbies and interests tell us a lot about who we are today.

Work with your quest box as much as you are able this week, but also keep using it, if it appeals to you, as you continue you on your lifetime intuitive journey.

18

what dreams may come

I am on a luxurious cruise ship, wandering through its narrow hallways as I frantically search for my cabin. During my quest for my cabin, I pass beautiful dining areas, magnificent lounges and showrooms, and opulent pools and spas. I pay these no mind, as I am desperate to find my room. Suddenly I realize that it is the last day of my voyage and I have spent the entire trip searching for my cabin. I have been so preoccupied with that mission that I have not taken advantage of any of the opportunities the ship offers. I have never eaten in the gourmet dining room or seen one of the touring Broadway shows. I have not been swimming or rested on the deck. Then I wake up. I know that I have just experienced an intuitive dream, and that I need to determine its message for me.

All of us dream nightly, although some people claim not to remember their dreams. This week, you will focus on your dreams. Our goal is for you to remember your dreams, determine which are intuitive rather than psychological dreams, and then interpret the messages you receive. I have never met a person who cannot remember their dreams if they intend to do so. If you are a person who claims not to dream, be aware that all people dream and that you generally have three or more dream periods every night. You do dream, your task is to recall the dreams with clarity.

In order to do that, you should first set your intention upon going to bed. Tell yourself that you will have an intuitive dream that evening, that it will awaken you, and that you will remember it. Believe that this is so for you. Don't sabotage yourself by doubting this intention. The key to remembering your dreams is not to move until you have transferred the dream into your conscious mind. When you awaken from a dream, don't turn over or sit up. Allow yourself to lie comfortably as you review the dream in your consciousness, going over all the details. At this point, don't analyze the dream, that will come later. Just commit the details to memory. Then, if possible, write the dream down. Many people keep a small light and a dream book by their bedside so that they can write their dreams down in the middle of the night. I have to admit that I am too lazy to do that. I have trained my mind to review the dream, remember the details, and then tell me about it in the morning.

The next step in the process is to determine if the dream is an intuitive dream or a psychological dream. Most of our dreams are psychological. Our brain uses our dreamtime to process issues, dump feelings, and give us insights into our behavior. These dreams are very useful when it comes to dealing with emotional issues. Analyzing these dreams can be very valuable, but they are not what we are looking for. We are dealing only with intuitive dreams.

So how do you know the difference? First of all, psychological dreams usually have strong emotions attached to them. You may wake up frightened, angry, or crying. Intuitive dreams seldom carry much emotion, although you will likely feel emotion later when you analyze them. Also, the content of psychological dreams usually has some relationship to what you are currently experiencing or feeling in your life. If you are fighting with your mate, for example, you may have a dream in which you are being beaten. Even though the assailant isn't anyone you know, the content of the dream has to do with your psychological feeling of being battered.

Intuitive dreams have a very different feeling to them. You might have an intuitive dream of being assaulted, yet wake up very peaceful and passive. You would know on some level that the content wasn't about "real time" events, but rather a message given to you with that particular symbolism. The final rule is to trust yourself to know the difference. Intuitive dreams feel important, but not emotional. If you set your intention each evening, then remember a dream, assume for this week that it is an intuitive dream and use it as such. The more you ask for intuitive dreams, the more your brain will supply them to you. Don't be disappointed if you aren't sure. Just use the dream you are given.

Interpreting intuitive dreams is not as complex as many people make it out to be. After all, you are intuitive and it is your dream. You will be given the correct interpretation if you let it happen. There is no need to run out and buy a book on dream interpretation or meanings of symbols. The symbols in your dreams are yours and will mean something very different to you than to me. When you have an intuitive dream, you must ask yourself this: "What do these symbols and messages mean to me?" You intuition will give you the correct interpretation. If you use a book or a friend or even a teacher, you may very well get the interpretation that is correct for the author or friend, but not for you.

My cruise ship dream is an example. Many of my dreams take place on cruise ships. I suppose this is because I have taken many of these voyages and they symbolize many things to me. For most people, a cruise ship dream would mean a voyage, an adventure, or a relaxing vacation. But, because I lecture on ships as a job, the symbol of the ship for me had to do with my work.

When I analyzed my dream, it was first clear to me that my intuition was giving me a strong message that I was so focused on a goal that I was missing all the fun and excitement along the way. The goal, of course, wasn't about finding a cruise ship cabin. So what was it? I sat quietly in a focus state and asked my intuition for an answer to that question. What I received was that it had two answers. One was just about life in general. My intuition told me that I was often so goal-oriented that I forgot to see the beauty and joy around me. The other was more specific. I realized that cruise ships symbolized fame and public attention for me and that my intuition was warning me not to focus on that to such an extent that I don't enjoy myself along the way.

When you analyze your dreams this week, follow a similar format. Remember the dream, write it down, and then sit quietly in a focus state. Ask your intuition what this dream means to you. Remember that some dreams have more than one level and that there could be several messages in the dream. You also may find that the analysis will come to you over time. You may find that you recall the dream unbidden several times over the next few weeks or months and that each time you receive new insights.

Don't take dream analysis to an extreme. I find that many of my dreams are what I call "dumping" dreams. My brain collects a lot of feelings and information over the course of the day and then dreams them away at night. In many ways our dreams act like a giant garbage dump, or maybe a recycling center. Our brains process what we need to know, then release all else back to the universe. If we didn't dream, we would go mad. Studies have shown over and over again that disruption of the REM state, which is when we dream, causes people to have psychotic episodes. We use our dreams to literally "clear our minds."

I have decided that many of my dreams mean little or nothing. Your intuition will tell you the difference between an important intuitive dream and a dumping dream. Trust it to tell you what you need to know. Then take the information you receive and use it in your life.

19

practicing precognition

I was standing at the counter of the District Court Clerk of Court office, filing simple divorce papers. At that time, a court appearance was required for all default divorces, and the final Decree was prepared and filed by the attorney for the Petitioner about three weeks before the hearing. I had done hundreds of these cases over the years with no glitches, yet, as I handed my papers to the clerk to be filed, a voice in my head said, "she's going to lose those papers." I ignored it and turned away. Never in my experience had the Decree been lost after it was filed with the Clerk.

The morning of the hearing, as I packed my briefcase and prepared for Court, I heard the voice again. Quietly and unemotionally, I heard the words, "The papers aren't in the file." This time I paused to consider what to do. I was teaching intuition training at the time and knew an intuitive message when I heard one. Still, I am also cheap and lazy, and making three more copies of thirty page documents wasn't my idea of fun. So, I decided to ignore this message.

You probably guess the ending to this story. The judge, in the demeaning way only judges seem able to do, looked at me over his half-glasses and said, "Miss Harwig, you forgot to file your papers." Of course, I stammered out my story, but only accomplished looking foolish in front of my client and incompetent in the eyes of the judge. And, naturally, it cost a lot more in time and money, not to mention pride, to make the copies at a public copier. All because I didn't act on clear intuitive advice.

A local newspaper once asked me to make predictions about various events and famous people at the beginning of a new year. I foolishly agreed to do so. The interviewer asked me a series of questions about celebrities and world events. I made some predictions but refused to make others. I wouldn't, for example, predict when someone would die, even for the sake of publicity. And, what I realized from that experience is that I really didn't care about Michael Jackson's marriage or the success of someone's political campaign. My interest in precognition is more practical. I want to know about me, my friends and family, and events that may affect my life.

Most of the time, you will be using your intuition to aid you in your day-to-day life. It is not that you can't and shouldn't help and care about other people, we will discuss using our intuition to help the world in later chapters. But, when you practice precognition, it is helpful to stick to issues that you wish to know for yourself. You can't do anything about an earthquake halfway around the world, even if you could predict it. But you can leave the house early if you intuitively know that the traffic will be heavy that morning. You may not care about an actress getting divorced, but you do need to know if your own spouse is unhappy. What you really want to know is this: Will the clerk lose those papers, will the bus be late, will the class be canceled? These types of precognitive knowings are useful to you. If you have that sort of information-and most importantly, if you act upon it, your life will flow more smoothly. You will truly have the intuitive advantage.

Precognition is just another variety of intuition. It is the one that most people think of when they think about "being psychic," for it involves making predictions about future events. Despite popular opinion, most intuitive messages are not about knowing what will happen in the future. I believe that the most helpful intuitive knowing is about ourselves, what we want, who other people really are, and so forth. Most intuitive knowing is really present, not future, time knowing. But, sometimes we really want and need to know what will happen. That it is when it is useful to practice precognition— knowledge of future events.

Before we go any further I must tell you that I do not believe that the future is set in stone. In other words, I do not believe in predestination. Therefore, all the future is change-able, depending on what you do in the present. No one, in my opinion, can tell you with certainty what will happen to you in the future. All you can get is a glimpse of a possible path, which is dependent on what happens between now and then. It stands to reason, then, that the farther in the future one gazes, the larger the margin of error. Remember that if you become afraid regarding well-known prophecies such as those of Nostradamus. No matter how talented he was at precognition, many events that he did not mention in his prophesies occurred between his visions five hundred years ago and the present.

"What good is precognition then?" you might ask. My answer is simply this. A lot of the time you will be right, especially when you are using your intuition for answers about everyday issues, such as parking places, financial matters, and appointments. Keep in mind that the more emotion-laden the issue, the less clear your intuition is likely to be. This week, as you practice precognition, stay clear of any issue that carries a heavy emotional load for you. You will be using your intuition for practical, non-emotional matters, for the simple decisions of life, remembering that life is really made up of simple things.

This week you will practice predicting. At the beginning of this week, list a few events or activities that occur regularly in your life. Examples are reading mail, answering the telephone, parking the car, taking elevators, going shopping, going to meetings, picking up your children from school, and so forth. From this list, pick three activities that you know you will engage in regularly this week; then decide that, before you do any of them, you will make a prediction as to how they will turn out.

Let's say that you decide to pick reading the mail, answering the telephone, and parking. For this week, before you read the mail, you will take each envelope (don't cheat and look at the return address), hold it in your hand and ask yourself what message it contains. You will write this down and keep track of how often you were right.

The same thing goes for the telephone. Each time the telephone rings, you will ask yourself who it is and what the crux of the call will be. When you park, you will ask yourself where, which row, which level, and when you will park. Ask yourself, "Of this bank of elevators, which will arrive first?" Before a meeting, ask yourself how it will go, who will be there, who will talk first, second, and what will be accomplished? How will your children's day go? When will they have difficulties? When will they be joyful? What will be on sale at the supermarket? How much will the bill be?

Keep track of these predictions and, if you like, create your own precognitive statistics. For example, you may find that you are sixty-five percent accurate in predicting parking spaces but only forty percent correct about who is on the telephone. Approach this week as a game you can't lose. If you want, you can even play a pretend (or real) stock market, picking a stock and predicting it's closing value.

The goal for this week is to see a concrete demonstration

of your psychic ability. Will you be 100% correct this week? Absolutely not. Will you get more hits than misses? I expect so. But, even if you don't, it doesn't mean a thing. The goal is the effort, not the result. This is a practice week. You are not trying out for a psychic hotline. Be gentle with yourself. Be impressed with yourself. And, when you realize how truly good you are at intuition, don't forget to follow through with it. Don't be caught without your copies made.

20

with a little help
from our friends

The power of group intuition is incredible to watch. You will find that, at least for some of your questions, your "psychic hits" in groups will be magnified many times over working alone. Often you will receive answers you personally would never have considered, and yet are incredibly helpful. Remember that your intuition receives messages from many places, people, times, and things. It is not nearly as limited as your conscious mind would ask you to believe. Because of this, a group "reading" is a powerful tool to put in the intuitive toolbox.

In many of my workshops, I use an exercise, which, to the conscious mind, would seem impossible. I first ask each person to write a question on a piece of paper for which they would truly like an answer but which they would not mind sharing with the group. I recommend to the group that they spend quite a bit of time honing their question so that it truly asks what they need to know.

Once everyone who wishes to has written their question (I never require anyone to take part in any exercise), we place the folded questions in a box or hat and draw one of the questions at random. I then ask the participants to pass the folded piece of paper around the room without opening it. Each person is told to hold the paper until they have a thought, mind picture, or feeling. They are then asked to write down a detailed description of this "message."

Almost always, one or more people report that they got a "blank"— no thoughts, no feelings, no flashes of insight. If that happens, I tell them to use the first thought that comes to them. Remember that it is almost impossible to not have a thought—the average person has between twelve and twenty independent thoughts per minute. This makes it very unlikely that these people did not have a thought. Rather, they don't believe that their thought or feeling has any relevance to the task at hand. I need to remind them that they don't have any idea what question they are answering, so they have no way to know what is and is not relevant.

After the paper has been passed around the room, I ask everyone to volunteer their answers. We write them on a whiteboard or flip chart. For example, they might look something like this:

Blue, NO! a white picket fence, a dog, happy, cold, an angel.

Only after everyone has had a chance to call out their answers do we finally read the question they have answered. Then, as a group we put the answers together to create a total "reading" for the questioner.

I have done this exercise with groups as large as forty and as small as eight (for this exercise, I believe an optimum size is twelve). Each time, the person whose question has been drawn has reported that the combined answers were very relevant and that the group interpretation provided the questioner with answers she would not have been able to get in any other way. Usually, the individual words mean much more to the questioner than they do to anyone else in the room. After seeing the words on a white board, the person for whom the "reading" is being done often knows at a gut level the answer to her question immediately, even without the group analysis.

There are always a few skeptics in the room, of course, who say something like, "Any free association of irrelevant words can be used to interpret any question." In a certain fashion this is true. Where else would this free association of words come but from your unconscious, intuitive brain? If you truly wish to discover your intuitive advantage, you must ignore this inner skeptic for a little while longer. The test of any intuitive exercise is merely this: "Does it work for you?" Like everything in this book, I am not suggesting that you use this exercise exclusively in making life decisions. That would be as misguided as not using your intuition at all. Give this exercise a try or two and make your own decisions about its usefulness. I think you will find that it can be a dazzling practice that truly must be experienced to be believed.

This week, gather a group of open-minded friends and tell them that you are practicing brain-expanding techniques. Then, go through the exercise as described above and see what results you obtain. You may be surprised at the insight you receive, not to mention how well you will get to know each other.

Sometimes, you even get answers to questions that you have not specifically asked. At one conference where we were practicing this method, we drew a question prepared by a woman I'll call Marge. As the question was passed among the participants, I was aware of a somber mood infecting the group. I asked to have their insights called out, and I heard things like, "healing, angels, hospital, peace, white light, dove," and so forth. It is seldom that a group has so many answers that seem so similar, yet when we read the question, the answers didn't really seem on point. Marge's question was, "What direction should I pursue in looking at a career change?" The group suggested to her that she might look at the healing professions, but she adamantly denied any interest or experience in that field. We were, quite frankly, stumped, particularly since she seemed very offended and defensive about the answers she received.

"Oh well," I thought, "sometimes this just doesn't work." Still, the next day I was not surprised to receive a telephone call from Marge. She apologized for the confusion, but said she just couldn't explain what had happened in front of that large of a group. "I did get my answer," she said. "The truth is that I have been diagnosed with terminal cancer. But I didn't want to talk about that in front of so many people." "Still," she continued, "the cancer is certainly the only question that is on my mind. The issue about my career was a smoke screen—and it didn't work. I received the answer that I really needed."

When you bring a group of friends together for this purpose, you will find that you are fulfilling more than one goal. You will, of course, get to practice group intuition, and you may get a very insightful answer to a question. But, you will also begin to come out of the closet about your intuitive quest. You may find that your friends and family are very intrigued by your journey and that they want to discuss ways in which they can join you. You will find, I believe, that you are not alone on your search for the intuitive advantage.

21

once upon a time

Many years ago, I attended a workshop put on by the writer and speaker Z Budapest. She conducted a fascinating exercise that I have since changed a bit and use in my own training. In this exercise, we were all given paper and pencils and told that we were to write a short story. The only instructions were that the story could only be one page long and had to start with the words "once upon a time."

After we had all written our stories, we rolled the papers, tied them with a ribbon, and placed them in a bowl. Then, one by one, we were instructed to ask a question for which we wanted an answer. After we had verbalized our question to the group, we pulled a paper out of the bowl and read the story. One by one I watched as each member of the group received a story which seemed to perfectly answer her question. When my turn came, I explained that I was a practicing attorney, but that I had been a palmist since I was a small child. I was struggling, I told the group, to incorporate two such disparate parts of my personality. I asked for guidance about this issue, then pulled a story and read this:

> *Once upon a time the pink ballet slippers were put on everyday. They were stored in a shiny, black case that hung in a special space in the girl's room. When they were new, they were a soft, vibrant pink. As they were used, they turned more gray, yet became more lifelike. Now the ballet slippers are gray and worn. Not having been used for so long, they have lost their life energy. The girl must return to the time and place where it is safe and good to dance. To lace up the ballet slippers again may mean a trip needs to be planned.*

At the time, this simple story was a great help to me. It spoke to me of returning to my childhood love of palmistry and, in doing so, regaining my life energy. Not long after attending the workshop, I was invited to a spa to read palms. It was easier for me to return to palmistry in a place away from home so, a trip did, in fact, need to be planned.

For this week, invite a group of friends to join you in a storytelling expedition. I love to do this exercise with a lot of formality. I like to use fancy paper and purple ribbon and a special "ceremonial bowl." But that is not required. All you need are a few friends, some paper and a willingness to try something new. Everyone loves a good story—this is an evening most people really enjoy.

Sometimes people are self-conscious about their writing or spelling ability. If this is an issue, the stories can also be spoken out loud. I do a variation of this exercise as a sort of message circle. Each participant is asked to write down a question on a piece of paper and place it in a bowl. Then we pass a "message stick" (any sort of stick or wand or other sacred item can be used) to a person at random, who is to draw a piece of paper, hold it without reading it, and tell a story to the owner—starting of course, with "once upon a time." Only after the story has been told will the question be read and the questioner revealed.

Children love this "game" as does anyone who is a child at heart. Some of the stories that have been written in my workshops have been truly works of art, although that is not necessary. The best messages often come from stories with just two or three lines but a powerful moral.

As you move toward building your intuitive community, it is important to find people who can share that journey with you. The experience of sharing stories can be healing and beautiful. Still, there may be some of you who cannot do this exercise in a group. Storytelling can still be an effective way for you to tap into your intuition. Intuition and imagination are strongly linked. Sometimes people who do not think of themselves as intuitive are strongly imaginative and love to tell a good story.

To do this exercise alone, you need to have a lot of questions in your "quest" box. Sit quietly, enter a focus state, and pull out one of your questions. Then ask your intuition and imagination to give you just the right story to aid you in this question. It is important that you try not to think about which question you might have drawn or what answer you would like to get. Just let your mind supply you with a wonderful story, then open your question and ask yourself how the story applies to it. I think you'll enjoy this week. It always reminds me of being a little girl and making up stories to entertain myself. Little did I know that I was just practicing my intuition.

22

psychometry

"Oh no," I thought, "I've finally done it this time!" It was my first chance to train police officers in intuitive techniques, and from the looks of it, "it might also be my last." Shortly into an exercise using psychometry, a young male officer was slumped down in his chair while being fanned with a piece of paper by his partner. "What had happened to them that could create such a reaction?" I wondered. The officer did look as if he might pass out at any moment. His face was ashen as he told the tale. I had asked each officer to partner up with someone they did not know well. They were to exchange personal objects such as rings or watches and then use their intuition to "read" impressions about the other person or object. I had chosen to do this exercise early in their training, primarily to get them out of their analytical mode of thinking. I hadn't expected great things at this stage but hoped to break down some of the skepticism and doubt that had met me a few hours before when I walked into the training room.

The shaken officer had been one of the most skeptical of the lot. He had the build of a young man who spent a lot of time lifting weights and working out. During my initial description of intuition, I had read a lot of doubt, even hostility, in his expression. Now, he looked confused and more than a little frightened. His partner for the exercise, a petite blonde with her hair pulled back severely into a bun, appeared to be more excited than fearful. She looked slightly dazed as they told the class what had happened.

Officer Mike started. "I have to admit that I thought this whole thing was a bunch of hooey," he said. "I never would have done this if it wasn't required," he continued. "So, I wasn't expecting anything when I gave Susan my car keys. She held them for a minute and then she tells me about a near accident my family and I were in a couple of years ago." He hesitated and then whispered softly, "But the weird thing is, she knew all about it—she saw the mountain road—even knew it was Colorado. She told me about the van, and how we'd just barely avoided going off a cliff!" He paused again, "She couldn't have known that, it's impossible." Susan looked up. "I didn't—honest!" She seemed afraid I would accuse her of cheating somehow. "I only met Mike a few months ago when we entered police training together here in Minnesota. We're not really good friends, I didn't even know he'd been to

Colorado." "It was a vacation." Mike interjected. "You couldn't have known. I'm sure I haven't told that story to anyone here. It was a long time ago and nobody got hurt or anything."

By this time, the class of forty or fifty police trainees was fascinated. I could hear murmurs around the room. "How did she do that?" "What did it feel like?" "It must have been a coincidence." "He had to have told her something."

The rest of the day went well, although without any more dramatic occurrences. After class, Susan stopped to talk to me. "What do I do now?" she asked. "How do I live my life knowing that I can do this?" A better question, I told her was this: "How could you live your life not knowing you could do this?"

Susan had just discovered her gift, a gift we all have—her intuitive advantage. She learned that she has the ability to know things without the use of conscious reasoning. Her life will never be the same again. She had seen a small glimpse of a skill residing within her, waiting for her to polish and perfect it. Now she had a choice. She could ignore this gift and pretend it never happened, or, she could study and practice and turn it into a tool she could use in conjunction with her logical, analytical brain to turn her into the best police officer, and human being, that she was capable of being. The choice was up to her.

Many of you use psychometry all the time, although you may never have had a name for it. Psychometry is simply reading the energy of, and picking up information from, material objects. A lot of us use it when we go shopping. You may have had the experience of holding something in your hand

and knowing that it wasn't for you. Or conversely, you may find that you need to handle all the vitamin bottles, for example, before you can chose the brand that is right for you. I find that I don't like to shop from catalogues because of this. I like to read the vibrations of an object before I bring it into my house.

The premise behind psychometry is that all objects pick up pieces of the vibrations or energy field of the person or persons that have been in contact with them. Rather like dogs that can smell things that we cannot (or think we cannot), we can pick up vibrations without being consciously aware of them. In the story above, the officer's keys were permeated with the energy of the near accident. Entering into a focus state and asking the keys to tell their story, the other officer was able to reexperience the incident.

Some objects seem to pick up energy more easily than others. Crystals and metallic jewelry seem to be particularly sensitive to energy vibrations. That is why most intuition trainers use jewelry or other objects worn or handled frequently as good items with which to begin. After you have learned the technique, though, you can get information from paper, leather, wood, clothing, and virtually any other material object.

This week, you will practice holding objects and asking them to reveal their secrets to you. Like all intuitive practices, you start by putting yourself into a focus state, then ask yourself what you feel, hear, think, or see in your mind's eye. It is helpful to do this exercise with a partner, preferably one who you don't know terribly well. That way you aren't coming to the exercise with pre-conceived notions about the person. Take an object from the person, preferably an object that they wear, use, or handle on a regular basis. Hold it while focusing and notice what feelings you pick up, what you see in your mind's eye, or what thoughts come to mind. If you don't "get anything," remind yourself that it is impossible to sit long without a thought, and use that thought.

Then, have courage and tell the other person what you received. Don't worry if it makes any sense or not, just tell the person. Encourage your partner to ask you questions so that you can elaborate on what they have seen. I once did this exercise with a young woman who claimed to have no psychic ability. I gave her a ring, which she held for a while and then said, "I don't get anything." Since I was teaching the class, I refused to take that as an answer. I asked her my usual question, "What would you get if you were getting something?" She sat for awhile, then answered, "I see a white house." I then asked her to enter the house. She looked skeptical, but decided to do as I asked. She then proceeded to describe my house, including the interior, down to the color of the walls. Finally, I directed her to ask the house if it had a message for me. She looked quizzical, but after all I was the teacher, so she tried it. She said, "It feels lonely." This reading was very meaningful to me. I had been traveling a lot and was wondering what effect my absence had on my life. I received an answer, even though I had to pull it out of her.

Instruct your partner to quiz you in the same fashion. Good questions to ask are things like, "What does that symbol mean to you?" or "Does the thing or person you saw have a message for me?" I think you will be surprised at how helpful this exercise is to both parties—and how much information you can get intuitively.

You can use psychometry in other ways as well. I use it a lot to practice my intuition. When I was a probation officer, my cases were first assigned to me by giving me a slip of paper with an offender's name and offense written on it. Before I scheduled the first appointment with this person, I would hold the paper and ask myself what I knew about him. (They were almost always men at that time.) What color was his hair? How many children in his family? Did he work? Then I would keep these "predictions" and compare them to the information I got during our intake interview. It was fascinating to see how often I was right, although I certainly had my share of misses as well.

This week, try this with any mail you might receive that you can't immediately identify. (Recognizing a bank statement doesn't count.) Hold the letter and ask yourself what is in the letter and who it is from. You can also use this at work with case files or personnel applications. You don't need to use this information exclusively, but once you discover how accurate it is, you will want to add it to your decision-making process. Use this week as an experiment in psychometry. Ask the objects with which you come in contact to speak to you. You don't need to let anyone know you are doing this if you don't want to—you can just let them wonder why life is seeming to go better for you lately.

23

psychic for a week

When I was a little girl, one of my favorite television shows was *Queen For A Day*. For those of you too young to remember, *Queen For A Day* was a game show where an ordinary woman would be picked out of the audience and, for that day, treated like a queen. She would be lavished with gifts, taken out for a fine meal, given a room in a luxury hotel, treated to a makeover, and so forth. Growing up poor on a farm in Minnesota, I watched that show and thought how wonderful that life would be. Nowadays, I sometimes give myself my own *Queen For A Day* experiences. I have created a life where I can give myself gifts, massages, and fine lunches—I don't need to wait for fate to choose me at random.

This week, you are going to give yourself a similar experience. You have been working very hard, and, I hope, having a lot of fun learning to hone your intuition. This week, you are going to create a life in which you use your intuition in your everyday experiences.

You can practice intuitive exercises forever but you will never get the intuitive advantage until you incorporate intuition into your daily life. For this week, you will crown yourself psychic for a week. At the core of your being, you will believe that you truly can know things outside of your ordinary senses, that you have control of this knowing, and that you trust yourself to act on this knowledge. Every morning this week, when you wake up, take a minute to remind yourself of this. Then, go about your daily routine. For the entire week, make every decision by consulting your intuition.

I am serious. Every decision. Does this mean that you can't use logic and common sense? Of course not. It simply means that you consult your intuition regularly, in conjunction with all other means you commonly use to make decisions. Unless you chose to do so, you don't have to let anyone know you are doing this. Intuition work is not very visible. You can be a secret psychic if you wish to. Or, you can boldly go forth and declare that this is psychic for a week time, and let everyone in your life marvel at your ability. That is up to you.

Start by asking your intuition what you should wear and what you should eat for breakfast. See if you get different answers than your usual routine. Ask for guidance on the route you drive to work and for the best parking place. Incorporate intuition into your work decisions. Use psychometry when you pick up a file, energy and aura reading when you deal with a client. Try to see your spouse or child by remote viewing. Write down what you see and the time you do it, then, later in the day, try to verify it with the person you viewed. Ask yourself who is on the telephone every time it rings. Predict things. Who will be at the meeting, who will say what, what is in this package? What will the lead story be on the six o'clock news?

Take your pendulum to the store with you to pick out the freshest vegetables, the best vitamins. Go shopping for new clothes. Instead of using only your eyes, use your hands and read the energy coming from the fabrics to pick out a new shirt or blouse. Go to the library or a bookstore; stand in front of a rack of books and close your eyes. Reach out your hands to the books and notice the vibrations that you pick up. Then chose the best book for you based solely on the reading you received from the book's "feel." As you read the book, ask your intuition why you were lead to this book and what messages it contains for you. Be brave and allow yourself to look a little silly. Why should you care if a salesperson looks at you inquisitively while you hold your hand or pendulum over a row of products? Just smile knowingly or nod wisely. It might just make that person's day.

Instead of eating when and what you always eat, ask your intuition to tell you when it is best to eat and what your body needs. Then follow that advice. Give yourself a week where you might eat ice cream for breakfast, or have dinner at 4:00 PM. Ask yourself why your body wanted a certain food. Ask your body how it feels after eating early or skipping lunch. Take a walk and ask your intuition to take you on the best journey. When you get there, ask what message you were meant to receive. One evening this week, hold the telephone in your hand and ask whom you should call. Then call that person and ask them what they need to say to you.

Be bold. Predict things for other people. Take your daughter's hand and tell her what she needs to know. Predict the game scores of your favorite teams. Watch a stock and predict what will happen to it. If you get an intuitive "hit" on someone, tell her, even if you don't know her well. If you need to explain, simply say you are taking an intuition-training course and need to practice. You will be surprised at how many people will be thrilled to hear what you have to say, and how often you will be correct in your read of that person.

The purpose of this week is to give you as much practice as possible in a way that demonstrates the concrete value of intuition. You are obviously going to be wrong a lot. And the point of that is to see that being wrong is no big deal. When you miss, just laugh and realize that being wrong teaches you just as much as being right. You are probably wrong a lot when you use your logical, analytical mind as well. All of us are.

Lighten up. Laugh. Enjoy. Psychic for a week is one of my favorite ways to break out of old patterns and see my life in new ways. I play it whenever I am feeling old, serious, or stuck. It never fails to help.

24

psychic protection

Laura is a well-respected and gifted professional intuitive and I was pleased and somewhat flattered when she asked me to look at her hand. I wasn't surprised to see how many small lines criscrossed her palm, but I was somewhat dismayed to feel the amount of psychic interference from others that she carried in her body. Just by holding her hand, I immediately felt anxious and out-of-sorts, as if a thousand different voices were vying for my attention. I explained to her that her nervous system was being bombarded by psychic impressions and that she was holding some of them in her physical body. She didn't seem surprised by this information. "I have been receiving psychic information from others since I was a small child," she explained. "I have consciously chosen not to shield myself from this information. Instead, I let it flow through me."

This is a conscious decision Laura has made, and, like all of life's choices, it has pluses and minuses. By allowing this information to flow through her, Laura functions like an intuitive river, literally being washed by other peoples' thoughts, feelings, and impressions. This gives her an amazing access to the pulse of humanity and allows her to do incredible work. But, in my opinion (and I believe she might argue with me about this) it also exposes her to the feelings and knowledge of others which she retains on a cellular level and which invade and confuse her own emotional makeup.

Many powerful psychics function throughout life with an underlying sense of grief. This condition has been present for much of my life as well, although since becoming consciously aware of it, I have chosen to cleanse myself as much as possible from the impressions that seem to give rise to this sorrow. These feelings are, I believe, an intuitive reading of the human condition and the state of our planet. Still, I am convinced that every psychic need not carry such a burden. I think that it is wiser to shield ourselves from information and feelings that we do not wish to experience and to cleanse our souls, spirits, minds, and bodies at the end of each day from those impressions which we deliberately picked up. Like Laura, we all have a choice not to do this. But, at least for this week, practice the shielding and cleansing exercises in this chapter. Then, you can make a conscious decision as to how much information you wish to pick up and how much you wish to retain.

Many of my clients are surprised, and perhaps offended, when I tell them that I remember little if anything about them after a reading. It is important for me to remove the impressions that are left behind after a reading, just as I would clean up dirty dishes after a dinner party. I do this in much the same way as I wash dishes—with running water and intention. After I have read a palm or have given any other type of psychic reading, I deliberately wash my hands, while creating an intention of love toward the person with whom I have visited, yet removing all trace of that person's energy field from my physical body. Washing your hands is quick, easy, readily available, and for that matter, a good way to avoid catching a cold. The key to this method of cleansing is to consciously intend for all energy which is not yours to be gently flushed away.

Water is my most powerful cleansing tool. I have found that a long hot bath does wonders for my soul. As I soak, I let the stress of the day drain from my body while I consciously release all negative thoughts from my mind. If I find that I am carrying any intuitive impressions from others within my body, I visualize them being washed away. I see them as an orange liquid that I release through my toes and then watch go down the drain with the rest of my bath water. I emerge clean both outwardly and inwardly.

I have turned bathing into a ritual of release. Certain soaps, powders, and oils have characteristics that aid in creating different moods. If you wish, you can add candles and relaxing music. I delight in the silence of the tub and have declared my bath time a sacred time from which I do not allow myself to be distracted. For this week, practice using water as a psychic cleanser. If you are not a bath person, use your daily shower to perform the same function. You can even search your body for old energy left behind years ago, and consciously release that down the drain as well. I suspect that you will feel better after a week of cleansing than you have for a long time.

Sometimes, however, the best thing to do is not to pick up psychic garbage in the first place. Many people are amazingly leaky, dropping their emotions and feelings like litter all over our planet. A few years ago, I was sitting in an airport at 7:00 AM waiting for a plane to Chicago. As I drank my cup of coffee, I was suddenly overwhelmed with a sense of anxiety and a peculiar urge for a stiff drink. I was very aware that these feelings came from outside of myself, and I looked up to see a woman with tense features walking past me. It was all I could do to keep myself from running up to her to verify my impressions. I didn't, of course, so I cannot be sure that my impressions were true of her, but I do know that I received a heavy dose of someone else's flight phobia.

I then realized that I had not bothered to erect my psychic shield, as I usually do when entering heavily populated places like airports, large city streets, and shopping malls. It was a simple thing to rid myself of her fear and took me only seconds to put my shield in place. But, I did need to take the time to do just that.

This week, make sure that you monitor yourself whenever you are in a place where many other people congregate. Some of the worst places for leaky psychic energy are those which generate a high amount of emotion. Hospital waiting rooms are notorious, as are government offices, courtrooms—and the neighborhood shopping mall a week before Christmas! If you aren't careful, you will not only intuit the emotions and fears of others, you might just carry them around as if they were yours.

In addition to learning how to psychically cleanse yourself, it is important to find your own personalized shielding method. First, you need to learn to identify feelings, thoughts, and emotions that are not yours. When you run into psychic litter, the most important thing to do is to label it as such. If you feel a sudden emotion that seemingly comes from nowhere, ask yourself, "Is this mine?" If it is not, don't hold on to it. Gently place the feeling outside of yourself or send it back with compassion to its original owner. You have no responsibility for storing other's feelings for them, whether they want you to or not.

Creating a shield is all about setting intention. The method you use is far less important than that you do it. Don't let yourself act as a human lightening rod, catching and absorbing the negative psychic energy emanating from other people. These people generally feel better for a time while you become exhausted and depleted. If you recognize this happening to you, you need to find a way to shield yourself from this unwanted intrusion and control when and where your psychic ability is used.

A client of mine is a very talented family therapist who had suffered for years from severe headaches. She came to see me for a consultation after having to take two months off due to her health issues. When I looked at her palm, I saw that her head line contained a mass of netting, which is almost always a sign of stress coming from outside of the person. "I have tried every herb and homeopathic remedy available," she told me, "along with all the traditional medicines. But, every time I return to work, the headaches return along with me." She went on to say that, despite her love of her chosen career, she was about to abandon it for good. I asked her to describe her work to me and was struck by one line she said. "All of my clients leave my office feeling better, while I feel much worse."

My diagnosis? A bad case of psychic littering and a worse case of lack of protection. We discussed a variety of methods of cleansing and shielding. Within weeks of implementing some of these techniques, she was back to work headache free.

There are many ways of creating psychic protection. Many people use prayer or visualization to create a non-physical or psychic barrier around themselves. First, visualize an image of something that you love that feels comforting and safe and that you can happily imagine surrounding you. Many people use white, violet, or blue light. Others imagine pink roses, white fluffy clouds or comforting, loving arms. I like the image of floating in a warm, buoyant Caribbean Sea.

Work with this until you find just the right image that feels good to you. Then, in the morning and whenever you feel vulnerable, picture yourself being enveloped in this substance. Visualize it as a permeable shield that allows what you desire to get through but keeps out all unwanted feelings, thoughts, and energies. Then, just as if you had sprayed on your favorite cologne, forget about it and go about your day. Without further thought, you will be sheltered and protected.

Some people also like using a concrete physical object as a symbol of their protection. If this resonates with you, you can shop for or make yourself a totem, perhaps a medallion or religious amulet to wear around your neck, or a crystal or other object to carry in your pocket. The important thing to remember is that the object in and of itself is not important or magical, it is your intention that makes it so. Holding it or touching it throughout the day will remind you to keep your protection around you. Other people create protection by smudging themselves with sage or other cleansing agents. What is used is less important than the fact that you take time to create a protective barrier between you and others. If you feel drained or exhausted after being in the presence of others, you have not taken the proper steps to defend your psyche from intrusion.

Use this week for exploration. How can you provide yourself with protection? How can you cleanse yourself? Are you surrounded by psychic vampires, people who deliberately or unconsciously drain you of your energy? If so, you may need to increase the power of your protection. The purpose of this work is not to make you feel paranoid or wary. The purpose is to give you control. Enjoy the process and make notes of what you try and what works for you in your intuition notebook.

25

creating community

Letting Your Soul Out of the Closet

For most of my life, I was a metaphysical loner, enjoying a solitary path in my spirituality. Since I was a child, I have had experiences and visions that I believed others would not understand or believe. The easiest route seemed to be to keep these happenings to myself. I was faced with quite a dilemma, therefore, when I wrote my first book on palmistry. "Should I use a pen name? How would my friends and law clients deal with discovering my secret life as a palmist? What would it do to my reputation in the community in which I lived and practiced?" As is true of most fears, these concerns were highly exaggerated. Most people, as it turns out, don't spend much time thinking about me at all. My book caused a small ripple of interest that faded after a day or two as everyone went back to their business.

My clients for the most part rather liked the idea of having an author for a lawyer, and the people who disapproved were apparently considerate enough to keep it to themselves. Still, I remained on the outskirts of the "new age" community. I have always been highly independent and have never cared to affiliate with groups or clubs. Still, the word community kept appearing to me—in books I read, out of the mouths of people I respect, and in my meditations. I felt led to examine my solitary pursuits and goals.

What my intuition told me was that part of my psychic journey is to help rebuild communities, not so much around geographical or political boundaries but rather based on spiritual and cultural values. Being an intuitive loner is just that— lonely. Much of intuition is about others, and the help and contact of partners foster all of intuition. There comes a time in all training programs when it is no longer enough simply to be concerned about yourself. In your intuitive training, that time is now.

As we embark on a new millennium, there will be many opportunities and challenges. No one person alone can affect the changes that need to be made to usher in the true Age of Aquarius. Nor will we comfortably stand alone to face the uncertain tides of cultural transition. Only in strong communities can we accomplish genuine change. I believe that the true goal of all intuitive practices is to make the world better for everyone, not just ourselves. The final lesson to learn in your training is the use of compassionate intuition.

I believe that you will find that the use of intuition without compassion will feel hollow eventually. I discovered years ago that I could train my students in all the intuitive techniques, teach focus and meditation, and see great progress made. But there was a missing link, a sense that there was another factor that I couldn't articulate and therefore couldn't teach. What was the element that brought all the practice and knowledge together? What made intuition into something different, magical? I now believe that the crucial element is compassion.

In my opinion, compassion is the key to releasing the full intuitive abilities of our brains. It is the crucial element that must be awakened and used before intuition will be anything more than a sideshow trick. It is the one thing that stops abuse of power, the brake on out-of-control use of psychic energy. Scientists tell us that we have full use of less than 1.5% of our brain's ability. The rest, I believe, is there waiting to be tapped when we evolve into a species able to handle all the magnificent power of our bodies, minds, and spirit with integrity and intent.

One of the best uses of compassionate intuition was communicated to me during a training program I was conducting for graduates of the FBI national academy. Martin was one of the attendees. A career police officer, he had been on the force of a major metropolitan police department for nearly thirty years.

When I asked the audience to volunteer intuitive stories, there was a long period of silence. No one wanted to be the first to admit that something "spooky" had happened to him or her. Finally, a voice came from the back of the room, "Ask Martin about the missing girl."

Everyone's eyes turned to Martin. He squirmed slightly and then told a tale that was infamous in police circles. "Several years ago," he began, "I was an investigator for our missing persons division. We got a call about an eight-year-old girl who had been missing for several days. The last time she'd been seen was when she and some friends were playing at a construction site south of town," he went on. "When she didn't come home that night, her parents and their friends searched the site thoroughly, as did the local officers the next day. Nothing showed up; she had disappeared without a trace.

"By the time our department was called in, all possible evidence had been erased by a heavy snowfall and further construction work. Nonetheless, we spent all day combing the site," he went on. "There was nothing to give us a clue to her whereabouts.

"I went home that evening, but I simply couldn't relax," Martin continued. "I just knew she was at that site. Finally, I returned to the area by myself. It was dark and cold as I wandered around aimlessly. I kept going back to a particular place. I know it sounds crazy but it felt as if I was being called to a certain spot. I just stood there waiting in the dark and the quiet—and then I heard a faint cry, coming from directly below me!"

Martin continued his story as the room grew hushed. "I was standing directly on top of her," he whispered. "She had crawled into a hole and a piece of heavy sheet metal had fallen over the top. Then snowfall had completely covered all signs of the opening. She'd been there for three days. I would never have heard such a weak call if I hadn't been standing immediately above her!"

Martin was uncomfortable with calling this an intuitive event. He did admit it was a remarkable coincidence or case of synchronicity. He also said he was more than a little bit tired of being teased about becoming the department psychic. "It was just a fluke," he said. "I'm really happy we found that girl," he went on. "But I sure don't want to do that again. It's just too weird for me!"

Without intending to do so, Martin had used many of the elements of intuition, and, by doing so, he had saved a life. First, he used intention. When Martin returned to the construction site, he intended to find the girl by use of intuition, whether he knew that or not. Otherwise, he would not have returned in the dark, when all other investigative methods had failed.

Another element of intuition is practice. Intuition is a skill, which, like all other skills, becomes better and better with use. As a veteran police officer, Martin had on many occasions used his intuition, even if he didn't label it as such. Some professions, such as police work, give ample opportunities for practice. It is much more effective, however, if you intentionally and knowingly practice intuitive skills.

Detachment also came into play in this case. In all intuitive work, it is important to remain unemotional and detached from the outcome. When Martin returned to the construction site, he unintentionally created a perfect environment for intuitive knowing. He went when it was quiet and dark, so that his senses would have less distraction. He stood at the site with a sense of detachment, not expecting anything but rather listening for an inner voice. He did not have any investment in this location nor any wishes or fears about the outcome. He was, although unintentionally, in a perfect focus state to receive information from his "blue" or sixth sense.

Most importantly, Martin was there out of a sense of compassion. He was not working the case for financial gain or notoriety. On the contrary, he was rather embarrassed to tell of his role in finding the girl. He went to the site out of a sense of compassion. This sense provided the trigger, which allowed him to hear intuition's voice.

And, of course, no intuitive practice is of value unless there is action. Martin could have sat at home and tried to communicate with the girl from the comfort of his easy chair. Instead, he left a warm dry house to stand for hours in a snow-covered lot. He made the hard choice to risk ridicule by taking action based on intuition. Intuition without action is a hollow lifeless practice, which will not provide the intuitive advantage.

This week, you, like Martin, will use your compassion to help others and to form or find a community of like-minded individuals. Intuition is certainly effective when practiced alone, but to fully embrace the intuitive advantage, I believe it is important to develop or find a community who will support and cheer you on in your quest for intuitive knowledge, and who will ask you to do the same for them.

The time has come, I believe, for us to come together in communities to explore and discuss our intuitive practices and spiritual yearnings. We need a safe place where we can talk about a sense of "being called to do something" without fear of being ridiculed or accused of having delusions of grandeur. We need a place where we can practice our intuition, feeling safe to be wrong, and affirmed when we are right.

These are days of uncertainty. We are seeing increasing numbers of people acting out of undefined fear—the fear of the unknown, the apprehension of the unpredictable. How can those of us who are on our own intuitive journeys combat the increasing sense of anger and anxiety that is already turning our highways into battle zones and our neighborhoods into fortresses?

Many of us have followed spiritual and intuitive paths for many years. We have read the books, attended the classes, meditated, and prayed. Now is the time for us to share our wisdom with the outside world. We need to bare our souls so that the millennium change will truly become a new age for us all. Yet revealing our soul paths is very frightening for many of us. I am constantly surprised at how many closet mystics I meet. People from every walk of life seem to show up at my office, often telling me that they were "told to call me" but unable to say by whom or why. I believe that we are being gathered as a spiritual force and that we will soon be given our working assignments.

Receiving instruction from an invisible force, whether you call it spirit, intuition, or God, can be very frightening. In my college psychology classes I was taught to believe that this was a symptom of psychosis—no wonder so few of us are willing to openly admit that we are feeling a call to action! Many of us have a legitimate concern of losing professional licenses, risking friendships, or even being locked away.

Still, I believe the time has come when the underground mystical and intuitive community must find its voice. We are hearing the still small voice of the soul—intuition, spirit—whatever we call it. So is the rest of the world. Imagine feeling this call without a vocabulary to name it or the wisdom to define it. Many people are acting out in inexplicable ways, partly, I believe, because they are hearing the whisper of spirit and it scares them to death. Violence, drug abuse, out-of-control spending, these are all ways that we deal with fear. But there is another way, a way many of us have discovered.

At crossroads times such as these, there is peace in knowing we are not alone. This week's assignment on your intuitive journey is to find or create a like-minded community with whom to share your triumphs, joys, and failures. You need a place to practice, a friend to cheer you on.

Every city or town, no matter how small, has groups of spiritual and intuitive seekers. Make it your personal quest to find them. Keep an open mind and explore this circle. If it doesn't fit for you, start your own group with your friends or soon to be friends. Then invite others to join you, even if you are afraid of their reaction.

Once you have found your community, even if it is only a few friends or family members, I urge you to use your intuition to help them and others. You will find ample ways to do this as you meet and discuss your practices and lives. Now is the time to reassess and then share your insights with the outside world. Tell your intuitive stories, even if you risk ridicule. Then invite others into your circles. Be brave enough to use words like spirit, soul, and intuition in everyday conversation.

This week, I urge you to let your soul out of the closet. The world will become a better place.

26

emotional alchemy

The first draft of this book was finally finished and ready to be sent to my literary agent when I took a break from writing to lead a group of spiritual seekers on a journey to Sedona, Arizona. While there, we visited a magical area near the small town of Jerome. We were in a place named Sycamore Canyon with two very powerful local Shamanic guides when, as part of a visioning ceremony, we were instructed to go off alone and invoke the four directions. I found myself in a peaceful spot near two large trees, a short distance from the creek. I turned first to the East, then to South, then stopped sharply and stared in amazement. A pair of fairies stood directly in front of me. But these were not the tiny Fey folk I remembered from my childhood. This couple was huge, well over seven feet tall, powerful and fully present. I could look at them straight on and they met my gaze with a magnificent and beckoning presence. Then they disappeared.

I was shocked. My logical mind couldn't grasp or believe what I had just seen. Seeing visions is always a little disconcerting, but I had grown somewhat used to that. What didn't fit was what I had beheld. I was in Arizona, working with Shaman. I would not have been too surprised to see Coyote or Kokopeli or some other Native American symbol, but fairies? In Arizona?

After the ceremony, our guides asked us to share our experiences. I was hesitant but finally decided to tell the group about the fairies. One of the Shamans looked at me and said, "You saw them?" It turns out Sycamore Canyon has long been known to be a place where the Fey dwell. For the rest of my time in the Canyon, I felt strongly beckoned to continue further downstream. When I shared this calling with one of our guides, she told me that the strongest fairy magic was about two miles further into the Canyon. But I was leading a group, and the responsible part of me brought the group out and on to the next site on our agenda.

After I returned home, I pondered what all of this meant. If my imagination was going to create a vision for me in that spot, I truly believe that I would have received one with a more Southwestern theme. The verification from the guide that fairies were known to exist in the Canyon also made me trust in the validity of the experience.

What then, did this visitation mean? I asked my higher self

and intuition for some insight into this. Why fairies after all these years? Why were they so big? And why did they now let me look them straight in the eye? My answers came slowly over a period of months, as I asked for and received insight. I was left with the question of what to do with this information. Did I tell anyone? My book was finished, and, anyhow, this wasn't exactly on the topic. Still, my intuition was insistent. I was to rewrite the last chapter and pass along the fairy wisdom.

What I was told was that spirits are returning in great visibility to our world because they are bringing messages to those of us who are willing to hear them. The earth is summoning her power and her friends and is beckoning some of her old allies—like you and me—to help her. In these days of increasingly aberrant weather patterns and natural disasters, the planet is flexing her muscles. The fairies, a symbol of earth energy, are becoming more visible, more powerful and more demanding. No more just gentle, playful, light beings, the fey are ready to become who they have always been—defenders and spokespersons for the world and all of its inhabitants. If we watch and listen, they will appear to us, recruiting allies in a time when Mother Earth is under siege.

Now I understood why this book had felt unfinished to me. The fairies appeared to tell me that intuition, spirit, our higher self, whatever we care to call that special skill we have been developing for these months, cannot be used solely for ourselves. We have discovered that we are all connected—that in some fashion, what is known by one person is known by all. Now we have to do something with that knowledge. It is not enough for us to use our intuition to pick stocks for our own portfolio and to tell us the best route to take to work. At some point, we need to use our gifts for the benefit of all things.

There are many ways to use intuition for the benefit of others, and I encourage you to seek out and use those ways. But I wish to leave you with a technique which I was given, in direct response to my questioning the meaning of the fairy appearance. This method, I was told, is so powerful that it can transform our world. It is called emotional alchemy.

As you have honed and practiced your intuition, you have also generated large amounts of emotion. We have discussed various ways of shielding yourself from the feelings of others and also ways of intuitively reading emotions. Now, you will learn to transform your emotions into power. Emotion, just like everything else in this world, is made up of energy. You can think of emotion as e-motion—energy in motion. Emotions are some of the most powerful energy sources on our planet. Our job is to take the unwanted or negative emotions which we all experience and learn to transmute them into positive energy that can be used for the benefit of ourselves, other living beings, and the planet herself.

I was given a very specific technique with which to do this. This intuitive knowledge came to me at a time when, for a variety of reasons, I was feeling a large amount of grief. There were times when this grief would hit me so strongly that I would become almost immobilized. I tried a number of techniques to distract myself from feeling so strong an emotion.

When that didn't work, I tried to release the grief to the universe. Yet neither stuffing the emotion nor releasing it seemed to be effective.

Then I was given the instructions for emotional alchemy. Rather to my surprise, I found that within a few days my grief had all but disappeared and, if it did return, I had a fast and effective technique to deal with it. This is the final lesson I wish to teach you.

As I have mentioned before, there are only two true emotions, fear and love. From these two emotions we create an abundance of variations. Grief, anger, anxiety, nervousness, depression and so forth all rise from the root emotion of fear. Joy, passion, happiness, creativity, and all the endless permeation of these, spring from the deep well of love we all carry inside of ourselves. The emotions that we generate are ours alone, and we are in total control of them. We do not need to let the energy stemming from fear remain in our bodies, nor should we release this energy to be endured by the planet. Our job is to recognize the emotion, name it, and then transmute the energy into love, which we then send forth to the earth and to others in healing and joy.

This, like all true wisdom, is not a new idea. The Taoist practice of the Inner Smile is a similar technique. According to the Tao, all emotions are lodged in various organs of your body. When you practice the Inner Smile, you first search out the locations of your emotions, then you "smile" at them, transforming negative emotions into positive emotion.

Emotional alchemy is similar. First you must spend a few minutes in a focus state, noticing your emotions. Then, it is important that you name the emotion. Are you feeling lonely, sad, angry, depressed? Put a title to your emotion and locate its source within your body. If you try, you will be able to feel the emotion in a particular area of your body. Once you have found the location of the emotion, sit with it for a minute, honoring it but not dwelling upon it. Do not put a storyline to it. It is not necessary and is counterproductive to spend any time thinking about why you feel sad, or with whom you are angry. All you want to do it locate the emotion and name it.

After sitting with the emotion for a short time, you will gradually gather it into a ball. As you pull the emotion tightly together, you gain control over it. Now surround this ball with light, transforming it to a brightly glowing orb. Visualize this glowing circle raising up in your body, flowing through your heart as compassion, and through your third eye (the area between and slightly above your physical eyes) as joy. Allow this love and joy to completely replace the emotion with which you started. When you are certain that you have completely transmuted your negative emotion into love, compassion, and joy, you then release this energy into the universe. Send it to the earth for healing. Let it flow to the damaged coral reefs, the oil spills, and the nuclear waste facilities. Picture this love encompassing whatever spot in the earth is at war. Transmit some to the latest site of an environmental or natural disaster. Ask your intuition to tell you where this energy is needed the most.

As we know from science, energy cannot be created or destroyed. It can, however, be transformed. Your transmuting of your emotional energy is a gift to the planet beyond measure. Still, you have not given away anything that you need for yourself. There is joy, love, and compassion in abundance left for you to send to any parts of your physical, emotional, and spiritual bodies that need healing. Do that now.

Recycling is a wonderful thing that we can and should do for our earth and ourselves. By practicing emotional alchemy you are recycling any negative emotions you carry into healing love emotions. In the process, you will feel better, lighter, and freer than you have in years. Your final assignment will last for the rest of your lifetime. Now that you know what you can do, you are to find out, on a daily basis, what the world wishes of you. And then, with compassion, love and bravery, you are to do that thing. How do you do this? When you wake up in the morning and every time you feel a fear-based emotion, transmute that emotion into love and joy. Then, spend a few minutes asking your intuition what it is that you are meant to do with that transformed energy. Use it not just for yourself, or even for your family, but for the good of the planet. Finally, send that recycled e-motion where it is needed.

As an intuitive master, you have a mission, as do all living things. This is not a burden; this is a great joy. Your intuition has been given to you as a way to communicate with your higher self for this purpose. Pick a time each day when you will spend a few quiet moments in contemplation. Look around your world, your living space, or the place where you are walking, and find an object that agrees to speak to you. Hold that object gently and reverently and ask, "What is my mission for today?"

Perhaps you will be taking a walk and you will see a rock suddenly glisten in the sun. Pick up the rock or lay your hands upon it and ask it what it has to say to you. You will get a message, either verbally, physically, visually, or emotionally. Trust that message and act upon that assignment. It may be very simple, perhaps merely asking you to lay your hands on the earth and send her some healing. Or it could be extremely tasking, asking you to change your eating habits or write a letter to someone who frightens you. Only you will get the message and only you will interpret it. But by now, you know how intuitive truth feels and you also know that it cannot be ignored comfortably.

Spend as much time as you can outside, listening to what Mother Earth has to say to you. We all have ancient memories of a time when the Earth's messengers spoke to us directly. The time has come again for us to learn to listen. Send the planet healing energy, and make sure to take some of her healing back within you. Use emotional alchemy to transmute any emotions that do not serve you. Do this every day, and I promise you that your life will change in wonderful and magical ways.

Finally, look for the fairies. When you go to the woods or work in your garden, keep an eye out for the fairies, gnomes, and elves. They are not just a sweet and simple tale from your childhood. They are also part of you, with a message you may wish to hear.

I wish you all the best on your intuitive journeys.

Kathryn Harwig

is an internationally acclaimed author, speaker, trainer, and attorney who conducts workshops and seminars on intuition, hand analysis, and the millennial change.

Kathryn appears regularly on television and radio and writes a column for a Minneapolis newspaper. In August of 1999, she was featured in a one-hour television special on the Arts Entertainment network's "The Unexplained." Her seminars have been presented to business, professional, and civic groups throughout the United States including FBI National Academy graduates, corrections and police officers, clerical workers, and business and professional groups. She is a former probation officer and has been a practicing attorney since 1982.

Kathryn's books: *Your Life In the Palm of Your Hand* (1998 Book-of-the-Month Club selection) teachers readers to learn about themselves by analyzing the shape, color, and lines of the hand; *The Millennium Effect* discusses millennial predictions and gives concrete suggestions for thriving in this time of change. Both are available from amazon.com and in bookstores nationally.

ordering information

To order
The Intuitive Advantage,
The Millennium Effect, or
Your Life in the Palm of Your Hand,
or to schedule seminars,
contact Palm Productions, LLC,
612-388-9220.

Visit my website:
www.harwig.com

To write, address:
Kathryn Harwig
c/o Spring Press
33 Fourth Street NW
Osseo, MN, 55369
763-315-1904